Supreme Instant Vortex Plus Dual Air Fryer Cookbook

2000 Days Instant Vortex Plus Double Decker Air Fryer Recipes It will be possible to create restaurant-quality delicacies in your own home.

Carol B. Grier

Copyright © 2023 by Carol B. Grier- All rights reserved.

The content contained within this book may not be reproduced, duplicated, or transmitted without direct written permission from the author or the publisher. Under no circumstances will any blame or legal responsibility be held against the publisher, or author, for any damages, reparation, or monetary loss due to the information contained within this book, either directly or indirectly.

Legal Notice: This book is copyright protected. It is only for personal use. You cannot amend, distribute, sell, use, quote or paraphrase any part, or the content within this book, without the consent of the author or publisher.

Disclaimer Notice: Please note the information contained within this document is for educational and entertainment purposes only. All effort has been executed to present accurate, up to date, reliable, complete information. No warranties of any kind are declared or implied. Readers acknowledge that the author is not engaged in the rendering of legal, financial, medical, or professional advice. The content within this book has been derived from various sources. Please consult a licensed professional before attempting any techniques outlined in this book. By reading this document, the reader agrees that under no circumstances is the author responsible for any losses, direct or indirect, that are incurred as a result of the use of the information contained within this document, including, but not limited to, errors, omissions, or inaccuracies.

CONTENTS

Introducing the Instant Vortex Plus Dual Air Fryer: A Culinary Revolution 9
- Advantages of the Instant Vortex Plus Dual Air Fryer: 9
- Usage Tips for the Instant Vortex Plus Dual Air Fryer: 10
- Cleaning and Maintenance: 10

Bread And Breakfast 11
- Frittata 11
- Strawberry And Peach Toast 11
- English Pumpkin Egg Bake 12
- Cheddar Bacon Frittata 12
- Baked Potato Breakfast Boats 13
- Spinach Omelet 13
- Mozzarella Chives Omelet 14
- Spinach Egg Muffins 14
- Simple Tomato Cheese Sandwich 15
- Mushroom Frittata 15
- Mozzarella Chicken And Pork Muffins 16
- Crispy Fish Sticks 16
- Mexican Breakfast Pepper Rings 17
- Mixed Pepper Hash With Mozzarella Cheese 17
- Baked Eggs With Mascarpone 18
- Pumpkin Donut Holes 18
- Banana-pecan French Toast 19
- Vanilla French Toast Sticks 19
- Asparagus Strata 20
- Kale And Potato Nuggets 20
- Italian Frittata With Feta Cheese 21
- Scramble Casserole With Cheddar 21

Appetizers And Snacks 22

Crispy Vegetable Nuggets 22
Squash Chips With Sauce 22
Herbed Pita Chips 23
Purple Potato Chips With Chipotle Sauce And Rosemary 23
Italian Dip With Cheese 24
Corn With Coriander And Parmesan Cheese 24
Cinnamon-pear Chips 25
Spicy Kale Chips With Yogurt Sauce 25
Apple Chips 26
Garlic Edamame 26
Potatoes With Bacon 27
Crispy Bacon Strips 27
Vidalia Onion Blossom 28
Cinnamon And Sugar Peaches 28
Crusted Prawns 29
Bbq Pork Ribs 29
Roasted Mushrooms With Garlic 30
Mayonnaise Crab Dip 30
Crispy Paprika Chips 31
Crunchy Pork Egg Rolls 31
Waffle Fry Poutine 32
Veggie Salmon Nachos 32

Poultry Recipes 33

Apricot-glazed Turkey Tenderloin 33
Garlic-basil Turkey Breast 33
Barbecued Chicken With Creamy Coleslaw 34
Garlic Chicken Tenders With Pork Rinds 34

French Mustard Chicken Thighs 35

Spiced Chicken With Pork Rind 35

Crispy Chicken Cordon Bleu 36

Tender Chicken With Parmesan Cheese 36

Cilantro-lime Chicken 37

Tandoori Chicken 37

Roasted Veggie Chicken Salad 38

Garlic-roasted Chicken With Creamer Potatoes 38

Crisp Paprika Chicken Drumsticks 39

Pecan-crusted Turkey Cutlets 39

Parmesan Chicken Tenderloins 40

Lemon Parmesan Chicken 40

Indian-style Chicken With Raita 41

Lemon-pepper Chicken Wings 41

Cajun Chicken Drumsticks 42

Chicken Wings With Lemon Pepper 42

Turkey And Cranberry Quesadillas 43

Roasted Turkey With Veggies 43

Beef, Pork & Lamb Recipes 44

Marinated Pork Tenderloin 44

Garlic Steak With Cheese Butter 44

Beef And Pork Sausage Meatloaf 45

Garlic Lamb Rack 45

Classic Spring Rolls 46

Elegant Pork Chops 46

Pork Chops With Sage Leaves 47

Crispy Mustard Pork Tenderloin 47

Spiced Pork Chops 48

Carne Asada Tacos 48

Air Fried Lamb Ribs 49

Super Bacon With Meat 49

Ham And Cheese Stromboli 50

Delicious Cheeseburger 50

Pork Chops With Rinds 51

Spiced Rib Eye Steak 51

Bacon And Pear Stuffed Pork Chops 52

Crumbed Golden Filet Mignon 53

Italian-style Honey Pork 53

Juicy Cheeseburger 54

Tender Country Ribs 54

Stir-fried Steak And Cabbage 55

Fish And Seafood Recipes **55**

Bean Burritos With Cheddar Cheese 55

Sea Bass With Greek-style Sauce 56

Typical Crab Cakes With Lemon Wedges 56

Buttered Shrimp Fry 57

Beer-battered Fish And Chips 57

Pasta Shrimp 58

Creamy Tuna With Zucchinis 58

Cajun Fish Cakes 59

Ginger Salmon Fillet 59

Snapper Scampi 60

Typical Cod Nuggets 60

Blackened Shrimp 61

Flounder Filets With Parmesan Cheese 61

Flavor Moroccan Harissa Shrimp 62

Parmesan Cod With Onion 62

Old Bay Cod Fish Fillets 63

Simple Fish Sticks 63

Grouper With Miso-honey Sauce 64

Spiced Shrimp With Zucchini 64

Tuna And Fruit Kebabs 65

Ginger Mushroom Flounder 65

Scallops With Green Vegetables 66

Vegetable Side Dishes Recipes 66

Sriracha Golden Cauliflower 66

Basmati Risotto 67

Creamy Cauliflower Puree 67

Lemon Cabbage With Cilantro 68

Flavorful Radish Salad 68

Parsley Cabbage 69

Curried Brussels Sprouts 69

Spinach And Cheese–stuffed Mushrooms 70

Cheddar Mushroom Cakes 70

Maple Glazed Parsnips 71

Gorgonzola Mushrooms With Horseradish Mayo 71

Apple Brussel Sprout Salad 72

Sweet And Spicy Tofu 72

Spicy Cauliflower Roast 73

Zucchini Tots With Mozzarella 73

Balsamic Sautéed Greens 74

Super Veg Rolls 74

Marinara Pepperoni Mushroom Pizza 75

Golden Pickles 75

Asparagus With Garlic 76

Herb-roasted Vegetables 76

Desserts And Sweets ... 77

Banana And Walnut Cake ... 77

Vanilla Berry Cobbler ... 78

Chocolate Peanut Butter Molten Cupcakes ... 78

S'mores ... 79

Air Fryer Reduced-sugar Cookies ... 79

Splenda Carrot Cake ... 80

Yummy Apple Chips ... 80

Vanilla Muffins With Pecans ... 81

Buttery Shortbread Sticks ... 81

Fluffy Strawberry Cake ... 82

Enticing Chocolate Cake ... 82

Chocolate S'mores ... 83

Cinnamon Pumpkin Cookies ... 83

Eggless & Vegan Cake ... 84

Banana Chocolate Muffins ... 84

Chocolate Peanut Butter Bread Pudding ... 85

Sweet Orange Muffins ... 85

Erythritol Vanilla Butter Pie ... 86

Cinnamon And Pecan Pie ... 86

Rich Chocolate Cookie ... 87

Fluffy Vanilla Butter Cake ... 87

Recipe Index ... 88

Introducing the Instant Vortex Plus Dual Air Fryer: A Culinary Revolution

In today's fast-paced world, convenience and efficiency in the kitchen have become essential. The Instant Vortex Plus Dual Air Fryer is a game-changing appliance that has taken the culinary world by storm. With its innovative technology and versatile features, this air fryer has quickly become a must-have for cooking enthusiasts and busy families alike. In this comprehensive guide, we will explore the advantages of the Instant Vortex Plus Dual Air Fryer, share some valuable usage tips, and discuss proper cleaning and maintenance to ensure your appliance remains in top-notch condition.

Advantages of the Instant Vortex Plus Dual Air Fryer:

Time-saving Efficiency: The Instant Vortex Plus Dual Air Fryer is designed to streamline your cooking process. Its dual cooking trays allow you to prepare two dishes simultaneously, saving you valuable time in the kitchen. Say goodbye to juggling multiple appliances or waiting for one dish to finish before starting another.

Healthier Cooking: One of the standout features of this air fryer is its ability to cook with little to no oil. Using rapid hot air circulation, it crisps and browns your food, creating a delightful crunch without the excess calories and unhealthy fats found in traditional frying methods. Enjoy guilt-free fried favorites like crispy french fries, chicken wings, and more.

Versatility: The Instant Vortex Plus Dual Air Fryer is not limited to air frying alone. It offers multiple cooking functions, including roasting, baking, dehydrating, and reheating. This versatility allows you to experiment with a wide range of recipes and cooking styles, making it an indispensable kitchen companion.

User-friendly Interface: The appliance features a user-friendly digital display and control panel, making it easy for beginners and experienced cooks alike to navigate and select the desired settings. Customizable temperature and time options ensure precise cooking results for every dish.

Family-sized Capacity: With its generous cooking capacity, the Instant Vortex Plus Dual Air Fryer can accommodate large meals, making it perfect for families or gatherings. Whether you're hosting a dinner party or preparing a weeknight dinner for your loved ones, this appliance has you covered.

Usage Tips for the Instant Vortex Plus Dual Air Fryer:

Preheat for Optimal Results: Preheating your air fryer for a few minutes before cooking helps ensure even cooking and crisp results. Most recipes will specify the recommended preheat time and temperature.

Arrange Food Evenly: To achieve uniform cooking, arrange your food items in a single layer without overcrowding the cooking trays. Overcrowding can lead to uneven cooking and less crispy results.

Shake or Flip: For recipes that require flipping or shaking, such as fries or chicken wings, follow the instructions provided in the recipe. This step promotes even browning and crispiness.

Experiment with Seasonings: Get creative with your seasonings and marinades to add flavor to your dishes. Just be mindful of moisture content, as excess moisture can affect the air frying process.

Use Cooking Accessories: The Instant Vortex Plus Dual Air Fryer often comes with accessories like rotisserie spits and trays for dehydrating. Make sure to explore these options to expand your culinary horizons.

Cleaning and Maintenance:

Proper cleaning and maintenance are crucial to prolong the life of your Instant Vortex Plus Dual Air Fryer and ensure its continued performance:

Unplug the Appliance: Always unplug the air fryer and let it cool down before cleaning. Safety should be a top priority.

Dishwasher-safe Parts: Most removable parts, such as the cooking trays, rotisserie spits, and drip tray, are dishwasher safe. Cleaning these parts in the dishwasher is convenient and efficient.

Hand-wash the Interior: Wipe down the interior of the air fryer with a damp cloth or sponge. Avoid using abrasive scrubbers that could damage the nonstick coating.

Regular Maintenance: Inspect the heating element and fan for any debris or residue. Use a brush or compressed air to remove any buildup. This step helps maintain optimal airflow and heating.

Store Properly: When not in use, store your Instant Vortex Plus Dual Air Fryer in a cool, dry place to prevent dust and dirt accumulation.

Bread And Breakfast

Frittata

Servings: 2 Servings
Cooking Time: 30 Minutes
Ingredients:
- 4 eggs
- ½ cup of cooked and chopped sausage
- ½ cup of shredded cheddar cheese
- 1 chopped green onion
- 2 tablespoons of chopped red bell pepper
- 1 pinch of cayenne powder

Directions:
1. Preheat your air fryer to 350°F. Lightly grease a 6-inch cake pan with some oil.
2. Whisk eggs in a large bowl. Add the sausage, bell pepper, cheese, onion, and cayenne powder, and mix until well combined.
3. Transfer the egg mixture into the prepared cake pan and cook in the air fryer at 350°F for 18–20 minutes. Check the readiness using a toothpick; it should come out clean after inserting in the center.
4. Serve with any fresh vegetables and greens. Enjoy your Frittata!

Strawberry And Peach Toast

Servings: 4
Cooking Time: 2 Minutes
Ingredients:
- 2-4 slices bread
- Strawberries, as needed
- 1 peach, corned and sliced
- 1 teaspoon sugar
- Cooking spray
- ¼ cup cream cheese
- 1 teaspoon cinnamon

Directions:
1. Prepare all the recipe ingredients from the list.
2. Spray both sides of the bread with olive oil. Place in the preheated air fryer basket and Cook at almost 375 degrees F/ 190 degrees C for 1 minute on each side.
3. Slice strawberries and peaches and prepare the rest of the ingredients.
4. Spread toast thickly of cream cheese, garnish with strawberries and peach, sprinkle with almonds and cinnamon mixture if you like.
5. Serve with smoothies, coffee or tea.

English Pumpkin Egg Bake

Servings: 2
Cooking Time: 10 Minutes

Ingredients:

- 2 eggs
- ½ cup milk
- 2 cups flour
- 2 tablespoons cider vinegar
- 2 teaspoons baking powder
- 1 tablespoon sugar
- 1 cup pumpkin purée
- 1 teaspoon cinnamon powder
- 1 teaspoon baking soda
- 1 tablespoon olive oil

Directions:

1. Preheat the air fryer to 300ºF (149ºC).
2. Crack the eggs into a bowl and beat with a whisk. Combine with the milk, flour, cider vinegar, baking powder, sugar, pumpkin purée, cinnamon powder, and baking soda, mixing well.
3. Grease a baking tray with oil. Add the mixture and transfer into the air fryer. Bake for 10 minutes.
4. Serve warm.

Cheddar Bacon Frittata

Servings: 2
Cooking Time: 15 Minutes

Ingredients:

- ¼ cup green bell pepper, seeded and chopped
- 1 tablespoon olive oil
- ¼ cup spinach, chopped
- 2 bacon slices, chopped
- 4-6 cherry tomatoes, make halves
- 3 large eggs
- ¼ cup cheddar cheese, shredded

Directions:

1. On a flat kitchen surface, plug your air fryer and turn it on.
2. Preheat your air fryer for about 4-5 minutes to 360 degrees F/ 180 degrees C.
3. Gently coat your air frying basket with cooking oil or spray.
4. In a medium sized bowl, mix the tomatoes, bell pepper, and bacon thoroughly.
5. Place into the basket.
6. Transfer the basket in the air fryer. Let it cook for the next 8 minutes.
7. Mix thoroughly the spinach, cheese, and eggs in a medium sized bowl.
8. Remove the basket; Mix them together and cook for 8 more minutes.
9. Serve warm!

Baked Potato Breakfast Boats

Servings:4
Cooking Time: 20 Minutes

Ingredients:
- 2 large russet potatoes, scrubbed
- Olive oil
- Salt
- Freshly ground black pepper
- 4 eggs
- 2 tablespoons chopped, cooked bacon
- 1 cup shredded cheddar cheese

Directions:
1. Poke holes in the potatoes with a fork and microwave on full power for 5 minutes.
2. Turn potatoes over and cook an additional 3 to 5 minutes, or until the potatoes are fork tender.
3. Cut the potatoes in half lengthwise and use a spoon to scoop out the inside of the potato. Be careful to leave a layer of potato so that it makes a sturdy "boat."
4. Lightly spray the fryer basket with olive oil. Spray the skin side of the potatoes with oil and sprinkle with salt and pepper to taste.
5. Place the potato skins in the fryer basket skin side down. Crack one egg into each potato skin.
6. Sprinkle ½ tablespoon of bacon pieces and ¼ cup of shredded cheese on top of each egg. Sprinkle with salt and pepper to taste.
7. Air fry until the yolk is slightly runny, 5 to 6 minutes, or until the yolk is fully cooked, 7 to 10 minutes.

Spinach Omelet

Servings:1
Cooking Time: 10 Minutes

Ingredients:
- 1 teaspoon olive oil
- 3 eggs
- Salt and ground black pepper, to taste
- 1 tablespoon ricotta cheese
- ¼ cup chopped spinach
- 1 tablespoon chopped parsley

Directions:
1. Grease the air fryer basket with olive oil. Preheat the air fryer to 330°F (166°C).
2. In a bowl, beat the eggs with a fork and sprinkle salt and pepper.
3. Add the ricotta, spinach, and parsley and then transfer to the air fryer. Bake for 10 minutes or until the egg is set.
4. Serve warm.

Mozzarella Chives Omelet

Servings: 4
Cooking Time: 20 Minutes
Ingredients:
- 6 eggs, whisked
- 1 cup chives, chopped
- Cooking spray
- 1 cup mozzarella, shredded
- Salt and black pepper to the taste

Directions:
1. Grease a suitable baking pan with cooking spray.
2. Mix the whisked eggs, chopped chives, shredded mozzarella, salt, and black pepper in a medium bowl.
3. Pour the egg mixture onto the greased pan and spread.
4. Cook in your air fryer at 350 degrees F/ 175 degrees C for 20 minutes.
5. When cooked, serve on plates.

Spinach Egg Muffins

Servings: 12
Cooking Time: 21 Minutes
Ingredients:
- 9 eggs
- ½ cup onion, sliced
- 1 tablespoon olive oil
- 8 ounces ground sausage
- ¼ cup coconut milk
- ½ teaspoon oregano
- 1 ½ cups spinach
- ¾ cup bell peppers, chopped
- Black pepper
- Salt

Directions:
1. At 325 degrees F/ 160 degrees C, preheat your air fryer.
2. Sauté ground sausage in a pan over medium heat for 5 minutes
3. Stir in olive oil, bell pepper, oregano, and onion and sauté until onion is translucent.
4. Add fresh spinach to a pan and cook for 30 seconds then keep it aside.
5. In a suitable mixing bowl, whisk together eggs, coconut milk, black pepper, and salt.
6. Add sausage-vegetable mixture into the egg mixture and mix well.
7. Pour the prepared mixture into the muffin molds and place into the air fryer basket.
8. Cook muffins for almost 15 minutes
9. Serve and enjoy.

Simple Tomato Cheese Sandwich

Servings: 2
Cooking Time: 6 Minutes

Ingredients:
- 8 tomato slices
- 4 bread slices
- 2 Swiss cheese slices
- Black pepper and salt as needed
- 4 teaspoons margarine

Directions:
1. On a flat kitchen surface, plug your air fryer and turn it on.
2. Preheat your air fryer for about 4-5 minutes to 355 degrees F/ 180 degrees C.
3. Gently coat an air frying basket with cooking oil or spray.
4. In the basket, place one cheese slice over one bread slice.
5. Then add 2 tomato slices on top. Sprinkle with salt and pepper. Top with another bread slice.
6. Insert the basket inside the air fryer. Let it cook for about 5 minutes.
7. Remove the basket; spread 2 teaspoons of margarine on both sides of each sandwich. Cook for about one more minute.
8. Serve warm!

Mushroom Frittata

Servings: 2
Cooking Time: 6 Minutes

Ingredients:
- 3 eggs, lightly beaten
- 2 tablespoons cheddar cheese, shredded
- 2 tablespoons heavy cream
- 2 mushrooms, sliced
- ¼ small onion, chopped
- ¼ bell pepper, diced
- Black pepper
- Salt

Directions:
1. In a suitable bowl, whisk eggs with cream, vegetables, black pepper, and salt.
2. At 400 degrees F/ 205 degrees C, preheat your air fryer.
3. Pour egg mixture into the air fryer pan. Place the air fryer pan in the air fryer basket and cook for 5 minutes.
4. Add shredded cheese on top of the frittata and cook for 1 minute more.
5. Serve and enjoy.

Mozzarella Chicken And Pork Muffins

Servings: 6
Cooking Time: 10 Minutes

Ingredients:

- 1 cup ground chicken
- 1 cup ground pork
- ½ cup Mozzarella, shredded
- 1 teaspoon dried oregano
- ½ teaspoon salt
- 1 teaspoon ground paprika
- ½ teaspoon white pepper
- 1 tablespoon ghee, melted
- 1 teaspoon dried dill
- 2 tablespoons almond flour
- 1 egg, beaten

Directions:

1. Mix together ground pork, ground chicken, salt, ground paprika, dried dill, white pepper, egg, dried oregano, and almond flour in a medium bowl until homogenous. Then add half the Mozzarella and using a spoon gently mix up the mixture.
2. Then brush the silicone muffin molds with melted ghee.
3. Place the meat mixture inside the molds, using a spoon to flatten.
4. Sprinkle the top with the remaining Mozzarella.
5. Before cooking, heat your air fryer to 375 degrees F/ 190 degrees C.
6. Place the muffin molds on the rack of your air fryer. Cook the mozzarella chicken and pork muffins in the air fryer for 10 minutes.
7. Serve the muffins at room temperature.

Crispy Fish Sticks

Servings: 4
Cooking Time: 10 Minutes

Ingredients:

- 8 ounces cod fillet
- 1 egg, beaten
- ¼ cup coconut flour
- ¼ teaspoon ground coriander
- ¼ teaspoon ground paprika
- ¼ teaspoon ground cumin
- ¼ teaspoon Pink salt
- ⅓ cup coconut flakes
- 1 tablespoon mascarpone
- 1 teaspoon heavy cream
- Cooking spray

Directions:

1. Roughly chop the cod fillet. Then transfer into a blender.
2. Place in coconut flour, paprika, cumin, egg, salt, and ground coriander. Then mix the mixture together until smooth.
3. Then place the mixture into a bowl.
4. Place the fish mixture onto lined parchment paper and then shape into flat square.
5. Cut the square into sticks.
6. Whisk mascarpone and heavy cream together in a separate bowl.
7. Sprinkle the fish sticks with the mascarpone mixture and coat with coconut flakes.
8. At 400 degrees F/ 205 degrees C, heat your air fryer in advance.
9. Using cooking spray, spray the air fryer basket.
10. Place the fish sticks evenly inside the air fryer basket.
11. Cook the fish sticks in the preheated air fryer for 10 minutes.
12. Halfway through cooking, flip the fish sticks to the other side.
13. When cooked, remove from the air fryer and serve with your favorite dip.

Mexican Breakfast Pepper Rings

Servings: 4
Cooking Time: 10 Minutes

Ingredients:
- Olive oil
- 1 large red, yellow, or orange bell pepper, cut into four ¾-inch rings
- 4 eggs
- Salt
- Freshly ground black pepper
- 2 teaspoons salsa

Directions:
1. Lightly spray a small round air fryer–friendly pan with olive oil.
2. Place 2 bell pepper rings on the pan. Crack one egg into each bell pepper ring. Season with salt and black pepper.
3. Spoon ½ teaspoon of salsa on top of each egg.
4. Place the pan in the fryer basket. Air fry until the yolk is slightly runny, 5 to 6 minutes or until the yolk is fully cooked, 8 to 10 minutes.
5. Repeat with the remaining 2 pepper rings. Serve hot.

Mixed Pepper Hash With Mozzarella Cheese

Servings: 4
Cooking Time: 20 Minutes

Ingredients:
- 1 red bell pepper, cut into strips
- 1 green bell pepper, cut into strips
- 1 orange bell pepper, cut into strips
- 4 eggs, whisked
- Salt and black pepper to the taste
- 2 tablespoons mozzarella, shredded
- Cooking spray

Directions:
1. Mix the all the bell peppers, pepper, salt, and the eggs in a mixing bowl.
2. Toss well to combine.
3. Before cooking, heat your air fryer to 350 degrees F/ 175 degrees C.
4. Gently grease a baking pan that fits in your air fryer with cooking spray.
5. Pour in the egg mixture and spread it well.
6. Top the mixture with Mozzarella and cook in the preheated air fryer for 20 minutes.
7. When cooked, remove from the air fryer and serve hot on plates.
8. Enjoy your breakfast!

Baked Eggs With Mascarpone

Servings: 2
Cooking Time: 3 Minutes
Ingredients:
- 2 eggs
- 1 teaspoon mascarpone
- ¼ teaspoon ground nutmeg
- ¼ teaspoon dried basil
- ¼ teaspoon dried oregano
- ¼ teaspoon dried cilantro
- ¼ teaspoon ground turmeric
- ¼ teaspoon onion powder
- ¼ teaspoon salt

Directions:
1. In a mixing bowl, whisk in the eggs.
2. Stir with mascarpone until homogenous.
3. Then add all spices and gently mix up the liquid.
4. Pour the liquid into the silicone egg molds.
5. Place on the air fryer basket.
6. Cook the baked eggs with mascarpone in your air fryer at 400 degrees F/ 205 degrees C for 3 minutes.

Pumpkin Donut Holes

Servings: 12
Cooking Time: 14 Minutes
Ingredients:
- 1 cup whole-wheat pastry flour, plus more as needed
- 3 tablespoons packed brown sugar
- ½ teaspoon ground cinnamon
- 1 teaspoon low-sodium baking powder
- ⅓ cup canned no-salt-added pumpkin purée (not pumpkin pie filling; see Tip)
- 3 tablespoons 2 percent milk, plus more as needed
- 2 tablespoons unsalted butter, melted
- 1 egg white
- Powdered sugar (optional)

Directions:
1. In a medium bowl, mix the pastry flour, brown sugar, cinnamon, and baking powder.
2. In a small bowl, beat the pumpkin, milk, butter, and egg white until combined. Add the pumpkin mixture to the dry ingredients and mix until combined. You may need to add more flour or milk to form a soft dough.
3. Divide the dough into 12 pieces. With floured hands, form each piece into a ball.
4. Cut a piece of parchment paper or aluminum foil to fit inside the air fryer basket but about 1 inch smaller in diameter. Poke holes in the paper or foil and place it in the basket.
5. Put 6 donut holes into the basket, leaving some space around each. Air-fry for 5 to 7 minutes, or until the donut holes reach an internal temperature of 200°F and are firm and light golden brown.
6. Let cool for 5 minutes. Remove from the basket and roll in powdered sugar, if desired. Repeat with the remaining donut holes and serve.

Banana-pecan French Toast

Servings: 8
Cooking Time: 10 Minutes
Ingredients:
- 8 slices of whole-grain bread
- ¾ cup of any milk you like
- 1 sliced banana
- 1 cup of rolled oats
- 1 cup of pecan, chopped
- 2 tablespoons of ground flax seeds
- 1 teaspoon of cinnamon

Directions:
1. At 350 degrees F/ 175 degrees C, preheat your air fryer.
2. Mix nuts, cinnamon, oats, and flax seeds into a food processor and pulse until crumbly.
3. Pour milk into a deep and wide bowl.
4. Soak 1–2 pieces of bread for almost 15-30 seconds per side.
5. Transfer the soaked bread pieces to the oats mixture and cover with it from per side.
6. Set the prepared soak bread slices into the air fryer basket in 1 layer.
7. Cook them at 350 degrees F/ 175 degrees C for 3 minutes, flip, and continue cooking for 3 more minutes.
8. Repeat the same steps with the remaining bread slices.
9. Serve with maple syrup and banana slices.
10. Enjoy your Banana-Nut French Toast!

Vanilla French Toast Sticks

Servings: 6
Cooking Time: 10 Minutes
Ingredients:
- 4 slices Texas toast
- 1 tablespoon butter
- 1 egg
- 1 teaspoon stevia
- 1 teaspoon ground cinnamon
- ¼ cup milk
- 1 teaspoon vanilla extract
- Cooking oil

Directions:
1. Cut the bread into sticks and keep them aside.
2. Beat the rest of the recipe ingredients in a suitable wide bowl.
3. At 400 degrees F/ 205 degrees C, preheat your air fryer.
4. Dip the bread sticks in the prepared egg mixture and place in the air fryer.
5. Air fry the bread sticks for 10 minutes.

Asparagus Strata

Servings: 4
Cooking Time: 17 Minutes

Ingredients:
- 6 asparagus spears, cut into 2-inch pieces
- 2 slices whole-wheat bread, cut into ½-inch cubes
- 4 eggs
- 3 tablespoons whole milk
- ½ cup grated Havarti or Swiss cheese
- 2 tablespoons chopped flat-leaf parsley
- Pinch salt
- Freshly ground black pepper

Directions:
1. Place the asparagus spears and 1 tablespoon water in a 6-inch baking pan and place in the air fryer basket. Bake for 3 to 5 minutes or until crisp and tender. Remove the asparagus from the pan and drain it. Spray the pan with nonstick cooking spray.
2. Arrange the bread cubes and asparagus into the pan and set aside.
3. In a medium bowl, beat the eggs with the milk until combined. Add the cheese, parsley, salt, and pepper. Pour into the baking pan.
4. Bake for 11 to 14 minutes or until the eggs are set and the top starts to brown.

Kale And Potato Nuggets

Servings: 4
Cooking Time: 18 Minutes

Ingredients:
- 1 teaspoon extra virgin olive oil
- 1 clove garlic, minced
- 4 cups kale, rinsed and chopped
- 2 cups potatoes, boiled and mashed
- ⅛ cup milk
- Salt and ground black pepper, to taste
- Cooking spray

Directions:
1. Preheat the air fryer to 390°F (199°C).
2. In a skillet over medium heat, sauté the garlic in the olive oil, until it turns golden brown. Sauté with the kale for an additional 3 minutes and remove from the heat.
3. Mix the mashed potatoes, kale and garlic in a bowl. Pour in the milk and sprinkle with salt and pepper.
4. Shape the mixture into nuggets and spritz with cooking spray.
5. Put in the air fryer basket and air fry for 15 minutes, flip the nuggets halfway through cooking to make sure the nuggets fry evenly.
6. Serve immediately.

Italian Frittata With Feta Cheese

Servings: 6
Cooking Time: 10 Minutes
Ingredients:

- 6 eggs
- ⅓ cup of milk
- 4 ounces of chopped Italian sausage
- 3 cups of stemmed and roughly chopped kale
- 1 red deseeded and chopped bell pepper
- ½ cup of a grated feta cheese
- 1 chopped zucchini
- 1 tablespoon of freshly chopped basil
- 1 teaspoon of garlic powder
- 1 teaspoon of onion powder
- 1 teaspoon of salt
- 1 teaspoon of black pepper

Directions:
1. At 360 degrees F/ 180 degrees C, preheat your air fryer.
2. Grease its air fryer basket with a nonstick cooking spray.
3. Add the Italian sausage to its basket and cook it inside your air fryer for 5 minutes.
4. While doing that, stir in the remaining ingredients until it mixes properly.
5. Add the prepared egg mixture to the pan and allow it to cook inside your air fryer for 5 minutes.
6. Serve and enjoy!

Scramble Casserole With Cheddar

Servings: 4
Cooking Time: 15 Minutes
Ingredients:

- 6 slices bacon
- 6 eggs
- Salt
- Black pepper
- Cooking oil
- ½ cup chopped red bell pepper
- ½ cup chopped green bell pepper
- ½ cup chopped onion
- ¾ cup shredded Cheddar cheese

Directions:
1. At 400 degrees F/ 205 degrees C, preheat your air fryer.
2. In a suitable pan, over medium-high heat, cook the bacon, 5 to 7 minutes, flipping too evenly crisp.
3. Dry out on paper towels, crumble, and set aside. In a suitable bowl, whisk the eggs.
4. Add black pepper and salt to taste.
5. Grease a suitable barrel pan with cooking oil.
6. Add the beaten eggs, crumbled bacon, red bell pepper, green bell pepper, and onion to the pan.
7. Place this pan in the air fryer. Cook for 6 minutes more.
8. Drizzle the cheese over the casserole.
9. Cook for an additional 2 minutes. Cool before serving.

Appetizers And Snacks
Crispy Vegetable Nuggets

Servings: 4
Cooking Time: 10 Minutes
Ingredients:
- 1 zucchini, chopped roughly
- ½ of carrot, chopped roughly
- 1 cup all-purpose flour
- 1 egg
- 1 cup panko breadcrumbs
- 1 tablespoon garlic powder
- ½ tablespoon mustard powder
- 1 tablespoon onion powder
- Black pepper and salt, to taste

Directions:
1. At 380 degrees F/ 195 degrees C, preheat your air fryer and grease its air fryer basket.
2. Put zucchini, carrot, mustard powder, garlic powder, onion powder, black pepper and salt in a food processor and pulse until combined.
3. Place the dry flour in a shallow dish and whisk the eggs with milk in a second dish.
4. Place breadcrumbs in a third shallow dish.
5. Coat the vegetable nuggets evenly in flour and dip in the egg mixture.
6. Roll into the breadcrumbs evenly and arrange the nuggets in an air fryer basket.
7. Cook for about 10 minutes and dish out to serve warm.

Squash Chips With Sauce

Servings: 4
Cooking Time: 25 Minutes
Ingredients:
- ½ cup seasoned breadcrumbs
- ½ cup Parmesan cheese, grated
- Sea salt, to taste
- Ground black pepper, to taste
- ¼-teaspoon oregano
- 2 yellow squash, cut into slices
- ½ tablespoon grapeseed oil
- Sauce:
- ½ cup Greek-style yogurt
- 1 tablespoon fresh cilantro, chopped
- 1 garlic clove, minced
- Freshly ground black pepper, to your liking

Directions:
1. Thoroughly combine the seasoned breadcrumbs, Parmesan, salt, black pepper, and oregano in a prepared shallow bowl.
2. Dip the yellow squash slices in the prepared batter and press to make it adhere.
3. Place the squash slices in the basket of your air fryer and brush them with grapeseed oil.
4. Cook at 400 degrees F/ 205 degrees C for 12 minutes. Shake the basket periodically to ensure even cooking. Work in batches.
5. Meanwhile, whisk the sauce ingredients; place in your refrigerator until ready to serve.
6. Enjoy!

Herbed Pita Chips

Servings: 4
Cooking Time: 5 To 6 Minutes

Ingredients:
- ¼ teaspoon dried basil
- ¼ teaspoon marjoram
- ¼ teaspoon ground oregano
- ¼ teaspoon garlic powder
- ¼ teaspoon ground thyme
- ¼ teaspoon salt
- 2 whole 6-inch pitas, whole grain or white
- Cooking spray

Directions:
1. Preheat the air fryer to 330°F (166°C).
2. Mix all the seasonings together.
3. Cut each pita half into 4 wedges. Break apart wedges at the fold.
4. Mist one side of pita wedges with oil. Sprinkle with half of seasoning mix.
5. Turn pita wedges over, mist the other side with oil, and sprinkle with remaining seasonings.
6. Place pita wedges in air fryer basket and bake for 2 minutes.
7. Shake the basket and bake for 2 minutes longer. Shake again, and if needed, bake for 1 or 2 more minutes, or until crisp. Watch carefully because at this point they will cook very quickly.
8. Serve hot.

Purple Potato Chips With Chipotle Sauce And Rosemary

Servings: 6
Cooking Time: 9 To 14 Minutes

Ingredients:
- 1 cup Greek yogurt
- 2 chipotle chiles, minced
- 2 tablespoons adobo sauce
- 1 teaspoon paprika
- 1 tablespoon lemon juice
- 10 purple fingerling potatoes
- 1 teaspoon olive oil
- 2 teaspoons minced fresh rosemary leaves
- ⅛ teaspoon cayenne pepper
- ¼ teaspoon coarse sea salt

Directions:
1. In a medium bowl, combine the yogurt, minced chiles, adobo sauce, paprika, and lemon juice. Mix well and refrigerate.
2. Wash the potatoes and dry them with paper towels. Slice the potatoes lengthwise, as thinly as possible. You can use a mandoline, a vegetable peeler, or a very sharp knife.
3. Combine the potato slices in a medium bowl and drizzle with the olive oil; toss to coat.
4. Cook the chips, in batches, in the air fryer basket, for 9 to 14 minutes. Use tongs to gently rearrange the chips halfway during cooking time.
5. Sprinkle the chips with the rosemary, cayenne pepper, and sea salt. Serve with the chipotle sauce for dipping.

Italian Dip With Cheese

Servings: 8
Cooking Time: 12 Minutes
Ingredients:
- 8 ounces cream cheese, softened
- 1 cup mozzarella cheese, shredded
- ½ cup roasted red peppers
- ⅓ cup basil pesto
- ¼ cup parmesan cheese, grated

Directions:
1. Add parmesan cheese and cream cheese into the food processor and process until smooth.
2. Transfer cheese mixture into the air fryer basket and spread evenly.
3. Pour basil pesto on top of cheese layer.
4. Sprinkle roasted black pepper on top of basil pesto layer.
5. Sprinkle mozzarella cheese on top of black pepper layer and place dish in air fryer basket.
6. Cook dip at 250 degrees F/ 120 degrees C for 12 minutes.
7. Serve and enjoy.

Corn With Coriander And Parmesan Cheese

Servings: 2
Cooking Time: 15 Minutes
Ingredients:
- 2 ears corn, husked and cleaned
- 1 tablespoon melted butter
- 1 tablespoon fresh coriander, finely chopped
- 2 tablespoons Parmesan cheese, finely chopped

Directions:
1. Butter the corn and then arrange the corn in the air fryer.
2. Cook for 14 minutes at 400 degrees F/ 205 degrees C.
3. When done, serve warm and top with the Parmesan cheese and fresh coriander.
4. Bon appétit!

Cinnamon-pear Chips

Servings: 4
Cooking Time:9 To 13 Minutes
Ingredients:
- 2 firm Bosc pears, cut crosswise into ⅛-inch-thick slices (see Tip)
- 1 tablespoon freshly squeezed lemon juice
- ½ teaspoon ground cinnamon
- ⅛ teaspoon ground cardamom or ground nutmeg

Directions:
1. Separate the smaller stem-end pear rounds from the larger rounds with seeds. Remove the core and seeds from the larger slices. Sprinkle all slices with lemon juice, cinnamon, and cardamom.
2. Put the smaller chips into the air fryer basket. Air-fry for 3 to 5 minutes, until light golden brown, shaking the basket once during cooking. Remove from the air fryer.
3. Repeat with the larger slices, air-frying for 6 to 8 minutes, until light golden brown, shaking the basket once during cooking.
4. Remove the chips from the air fryer. Cool and serve or store in an airtight container at room temperature up for to 2 days.

Spicy Kale Chips With Yogurt Sauce

Servings:4
Cooking Time: 5 Minutes
Ingredients:
- 1 cup Greek yogurt
- 3 tablespoons lemon juice
- 2 tablespoons honey mustard
- ½ teaspoon dried oregano
- 1 bunch curly kale
- 2 tablespoons olive oil
- ½ teaspoon salt
- ⅛ teaspoon pepper

Directions:
1. In a small bowl, combine the yogurt, lemon juice, honey mustard, and oregano, and set aside.
2. Remove the stems and ribs from the kale with a sharp knife. Cut the leaves into 2- to 3-inch pieces.
3. Toss the kale with olive oil, salt, and pepper. Massage the oil into the leaves with your hands.
4. Air-fry the kale in batches until crisp, about 5 minutes, shaking the basket once during cooking time. Serve with the yogurt sauce.

Apple Chips

Servings: 4
Cooking Time: 10 Minutes
Ingredients:
- 4 medium apples (any type will work), cored
- ¼ teaspoon cinnamon
- ¼ teaspoon nutmeg

Directions:
1. Cut the apples into ⅓-inch-thick slices. Thin slices yield crunchy chips.
2. Place the apple slices in a large bowl. Sprinkle the cinnamon and nutmeg onto the apple slices.
3. Transfer the apple chips to the air fryer. It is okay to stack them. Cook for 6 minutes.
4. Open the air fryer and shake the basket. Cook for an additional 4 minutes, or until crunchy.
5. Cool before serving.

Garlic Edamame

Servings: 4
Cooking Time: 10 Minutes
Ingredients:
- Olive oil
- 1 (16-ounce) bag frozen edamame in pods
- ½ teaspoon salt
- ½ teaspoon garlic salt
- ¼ teaspoon freshly ground black pepper
- ½ teaspoon red pepper flakes (optional)

Directions:
1. Spray a fryer basket lightly with olive oil.
2. In a medium bowl, add the frozen edamame and lightly spray with olive oil. Toss to coat.
3. In a small bowl, mix together the salt, garlic salt, black pepper, and red pepper flakes (if using). Add the mixture to the edamame and toss until evenly coated.
4. Place half the edamame in the fryer basket. Do not overfill the basket.
5. Air fry for 5 minutes. Shake the basket and cook until the edamame is starting to brown and get crispy, 3 to 5 more minutes.
6. Repeat with the remaining edamame and serve immediately.

Potatoes With Bacon

Servings: 4
Cooking Time: 30 Minutes
Ingredients:
- 4 potatoes, scrubbed, halved, cut lengthwise
- 1 tbsp. olive oil
- Salt and black pepper to taste
- 4 oz. bacon, chopped

Directions:
1. Brush the potatoes with olive oil and season with salt and pepper.
2. Transfer the seasoned potatoes to the cooking basket and arrange it to your air fryer.
3. Cook them at 390 degrees F/ 200 degrees C for 30 minutes, flipping and topping with bacon halfway through the cooking time.
4. When done, serve and enjoy.

Crispy Bacon Strips

Servings: 4
Cooking Time: 10 Minutes
Ingredients:
- 4 bacon strips, cut into small pieces
- ½ cup pork rinds, crushed
- ¼ cup hot sauce

Directions:
1. Add bacon pieces in a suitable bowl.
2. Add hot sauce and toss well.
3. Add crushed pork rinds and toss until bacon pieces are well coated.
4. Transfer bacon pieces in air fryer basket and cook at almost 350 degrees F/ 175 degrees C for almost 10 minutes.
5. Serve and enjoy.

Vidalia Onion Blossom

Servings: 4
Cooking Time: 25 Minutes
Ingredients:

- 1 large Vidalia onion
- 1½ cups all-purpose flour
- 1 teaspoon garlic powder
- 1 teaspoon paprika
- Salt
- Pepper
- 2 eggs
- 1 cup milk
- Cooking oil

Directions:

1. Cut off the pointy stem end of the onion. Leave the root end intact. Peel the onion and place it cut-side down. The root end of the onion should be facing up.
2. Starting about ½ inch from the root end, cut downward to make 4 evenly spaced cuts. In each section, make 3 additional cuts. There should be 16 cuts in the onion.
3. Turn the onion over and fluff out the "petals."
4. Place the flour in a large bowl and season it with the garlic powder, paprika, and salt and pepper to taste.
5. In another large bowl, whisk the eggs. Add the milk and stir. This will form a batter.
6. Place the onion in the bowl with the flour mixture. Use a large spoon to cover the onion petals in flour.
7. Transfer the onion to the batter. Use a spoon or basting brush to cover the onion completely.
8. Return the onion to the flour mixture. Cover completely.
9. Wrap the battered onion in foil and place in the freezer for 45 minutes.
10. Spray the air fryer basket with cooking oil. Unwrap the foil covering and place the onion in the air fryer basket. Cook for 10 minutes.
11. Open the air fryer. Spray the onion with cooking oil. If areas of the onion are still white from the flour, focus the spray on these areas.
12. Cook for an additional 10 to 15 minutes, or until crisp.

Cinnamon And Sugar Peaches

Servings: 4
Cooking Time: 13 Minutes
Ingredients:

- Olive oil
- 2 tablespoons sugar
- ¼ teaspoon ground cinnamon
- 4 peaches, cut into wedges

Directions:

1. Spray a fryer basket lightly with olive oil.
2. In a medium bowl, combine the sugar and cinnamon. Add the peaches and toss to coat evenly.
3. Place the peaches in a single layer in the fryer basket on their sides. You may need to cook them in batches.
4. Air fry for 5 minutes. Turn the peaches skin side down, lightly spray them with oil, and air fry until the peaches are lightly brown and caramelized, 5 to 8 more minutes.

Crusted Prawns

Servings: 4
Cooking Time: 8 Minutes
Ingredients:
- 1 egg
- ½ pound nacho chips, crushed
- 18 prawns, peeled and deveined

Directions:
1. In a shallow dish, crack the egg, and beat well.
2. Put the crushed nacho chips in another dish.
3. Now, dip the prawn into beaten egg and then, coat with the nacho chips.
4. At 355 degrees F/ 180 degrees C, preheat your air fryer.
5. Place the prepared prawns in the air fryer basket in a single layer.
6. Air fry for about 8 minutes.
7. Serve hot.

Bbq Pork Ribs

Servings: 2
Cooking Time: 35 Minutes
Ingredients:
- 1 tablespoon kosher salt
- 1 tablespoon dark brown sugar
- 1 tablespoon sweet paprika
- 1 teaspoon garlic powder
- 1 teaspoon onion powder
- 1 teaspoon poultry seasoning
- ½ teaspoon mustard powder
- ½ teaspoon freshly ground black pepper
- 2¼ pounds (1 kg) individually cut St. Louis–style pork spareribs

Directions:
1. Preheat the air fryer to 350ºF (177ºC).
2. In a large bowl, whisk together the salt, brown sugar, paprika, garlic powder, onion powder, poultry seasoning, mustard powder, and pepper. Add the ribs and toss. Rub the seasonings into them with your hands until they're fully coated.
3. Arrange the ribs in the air fryer basket, standing up on their ends and leaned up against the wall of the basket and each other. Roast for 35 minutes, or until the ribs are tender inside and golden brown and crisp on the outside. Transfer the ribs to plates and serve hot.

Roasted Mushrooms With Garlic

Servings: 4
Cooking Time: 22 To 27 Minutes

Ingredients:
- 16 garlic cloves, peeled (see Tip)
- 2 teaspoons olive oil, divided
- 16 button mushrooms
- ½ teaspoon dried marjoram
- ⅛ teaspoon freshly ground black pepper
- 1 tablespoon white wine or low-sodium vegetable broth

Directions:
1. In a 6-by-2-inch pan, mix the garlic with 1 teaspoon of olive oil. Roast in the air fryer for 12 minutes.
2. Add the mushrooms, marjoram, and pepper. Stir to coat. Drizzle with the remaining 1 teaspoon of olive oil and the white wine.
3. Return to the air fryer and roast for 10 to 15 minutes more, or until the mushrooms and garlic cloves are tender. Serve.

Mayonnaise Crab Dip

Servings: 4
Cooking Time: 7 Minutes

Ingredients:
- 1 cup crabmeat
- 2 tablespoons parsley, chopped
- 2 tablespoons fresh lemon juice
- 2 tablespoons hot sauce
- ½ cup green onion, sliced
- 2 cups cheese, grated
- ¼ cup mayonnaise
- ¼ teaspoon black pepper
- ½ teaspoon salt

Directions:
1. In a 6-inch dish, mix together crabmeat, hot sauce, cheese, mayo, black pepper, and salt.
2. Place dish in air fryer basket and cook dip at 400 degrees F/ 205 degrees C for 7 minutes.
3. Remove dish from the air fryer.
4. Drizzle dip with lemon juice and garnish with parsley.
5. Serve and enjoy.

Crispy Paprika Chips

Servings: 4
Cooking Time: 5 Minutes
Ingredients:
- 8 ounces' cheddar cheese, shredded
- 1 teaspoon sweet paprika

Directions:
1. Divide the cheese in small heaps in a suitable pan.
2. After sprinkling the paprika on top, arrange the cheeses to the air fryer and cook at 400 degrees F/ 205 degrees C for 5 minutes.
3. Cool the chips down before serving them.

Crunchy Pork Egg Rolls

Servings: 12
Cooking Time: 15 Minutes
Ingredients:
- Cooking oil
- 2 garlic cloves, minced
- 1 teaspoon sesame oil
- ¼ cup soy sauce
- 2 teaspoons grated fresh ginger
- 12 ounces ground pork
- ½ cabbage, shredded (2 cups)
- 4 scallions, green parts (white parts optional), chopped
- 24 egg roll wrappers

Directions:
1. Spray a skillet with cooking oil and place over medium-high heat. Add the garlic. Cook for 1 minute, until fragrant.
2. Add the ground pork to the skillet. Using a spoon, break the pork into smaller chunks.
3. In a small bowl, combine the sesame oil, soy sauce, and ginger. Mix well to combine.
4. Add the sauce to the skillet. Stir to combine. Continue cooking for 5 minutes, until the pork is browned.
5. When the pork has browned, add the cabbage and scallions. Mix well.
6. Transfer the pork mixture to a large bowl.
7. Lay the egg roll wrappers on a flat surface. Dip a basting brush in water and glaze each of the egg roll wrappers along the edges with the wet brush. This will soften the dough and make it easier to roll.
8. Stack 2 egg roll wrappers (it works best if you double-wrap the egg rolls). Scoop 1 to 2 tablespoons of the pork mixture onto the center.
9. Roll one long side of the wrappers up over the filling. Press firmly on the area with the filling, tucking it in lightly to secure it in place. Next, fold in the left and right sides.
10. Continue rolling to close. Use the basting brush to wet the seam and seal the egg roll.
11. Place the egg rolls in the basket of the air fryer. It is okay to stack them. Spray them with cooking oil. Cook for 8 minutes.
12. Flip the egg rolls. Cook for an additional 4 minutes.
13. Cool before serving.

Waffle Fry Poutine

Servings: 4
Cooking Time: 15 To 17 Minutes
Ingredients:
- 2 cups frozen waffle cut fries
- 2 teaspoons olive oil
- 1 red bell pepper, chopped
- 2 green onions, sliced
- 1 cup shredded Swiss cheese
- ½ cup bottled chicken gravy

Directions:
1. Toss the waffle fries with olive oil and place in the air fryer basket. Air-fry for 10 to 12 minutes or until the fries are crisp and light golden brown, shaking the basket halfway through the cooking time.
2. Transfer the fries to a 6-by-6-by-2-inch pan and top with the pepper, green onions, and cheese. Air-fry for 3 minutes until the vegetables are crisp and tender.
3. Remove the pan from the air fryer and drizzle the gravy over the fries. Air-fry for 2 minutes or until the gravy is hot. Serve immediately.

Veggie Salmon Nachos

Servings: 6
Cooking Time: 9 To 12 Minutes
Ingredients:
- 2 ounces (57 g) baked no-salt corn tortilla chips
- 1 (5-ounce / 142-g) baked salmon fillet, flaked
- ½ cup canned low-sodium black beans, rinsed and drained
- 1 red bell pepper, chopped
- ½ cup grated carrot
- 1 jalapeño pepper, minced
- ⅓ cup shredded low-sodium low-fat Swiss cheese
- 1 tomato, chopped

Directions:
1. Preheat the air fryer to 360°F (182°C).
2. In a baking pan, layer the tortilla chips. Top with the salmon, black beans, red bell pepper, carrot, jalapeño, and Swiss cheese.
3. Bake in the air fryer for 9 to 12 minutes, or until the cheese is melted and starts to brown.
4. Top with the tomato and serve.

Poultry Recipes
Apricot-glazed Turkey Tenderloin

Servings:4
Cooking Time: 30 Minutes
Ingredients:
- Olive oil
- ¼ cup sugar-free apricot preserves
- ½ tablespoon spicy brown mustard
- 1½ pound turkey breast tenderloin
- Salt
- Freshly ground black pepper

Directions:
1. Spray a fryer basket lightly with olive oil.
2. In a small bowl, combine the apricot preserves and mustard to make a paste.
3. Season the turkey with salt and pepper. Spread the apricot paste all over the turkey.
4. Place the turkey in the fryer basket and lightly spray with olive oil.
5. Air fry for 15 minutes. Flip the turkey over and lightly spray with olive oil. Air fry until the internal temperature reaches at least 170°F, an additional 10 to 15 minutes.
6. Let the turkey rest for 10 minutes before slicing and serving.

Garlic-basil Turkey Breast

Servings: 4
Cooking Time: 42 Minutes
Ingredients:
- 1 ½ pounds turkey breast
- 2 tablespoons olive oil
- 2 cloves garlic, minced
- Sea salt, to taste
- Ground black pepper, to taste
- 1 teaspoon basil
- 2 tablespoons lemon zest, grated

Directions:
1. Using paper towels pat dry the turkey breast.
2. Toss the turkey breast with salt, pepper, lemon zest, basil, garlic, and olive oil.
3. Before cooking, heat your air fryer to 380 degrees F/ 195 degrees C.
4. Arrange the chicken breast inside the air fryer basket.
5. Cook in your air fryer for 20 minutes.
6. Then flip the turkey breast and cook for 20 to 22 minutes.
7. Enjoy!

Barbecued Chicken With Creamy Coleslaw

Servings: 2
Cooking Time: 20 Minutes
Ingredients:

- 3 cups shredded coleslaw mix
- Salt and pepper
- 2 (12-ounce / 340-g) bone-in split chicken breasts, trimmed
- 1 teaspoon vegetable oil
- 2 tablespoons barbecue sauce, plus extra for serving
- 2 tablespoons mayonnaise
- 2 tablespoons sour cream
- 1 teaspoon distilled white vinegar, plus extra for seasoning
- ¼ teaspoon sugar

Directions:

1. Preheat the air fryer to 350ºF (177ºC).
2. Toss coleslaw mix and ¼ teaspoon salt in a colander set over bowl. Let sit until wilted slightly, about 30 minutes. Rinse, drain, and dry well with a dish towel.
3. Meanwhile, pat chicken dry with paper towels, rub with oil, and season with salt and pepper. Arrange breasts skin-side down in air fryer basket, spaced evenly apart, alternating ends. Bake for 10 minutes. Flip breasts and brush skin side with barbecue sauce. Return basket to air fryer and bake until well browned and chicken registers 160ºF (71ºC), 10 to 15 minutes.
4. Transfer chicken to serving platter, tent loosely with aluminum foil, and let rest for 5 minutes. While chicken rests, whisk mayonnaise, sour cream, vinegar, sugar, and pinch pepper together in a large bowl. Stir in coleslaw mix and season with salt, pepper, and additional vinegar to taste. Serve chicken with coleslaw, passing extra barbecue sauce separately.

Garlic Chicken Tenders With Pork Rinds

Servings: 4
Cooking Time: 20 Minutes
Ingredients:

- 1-pound boneless, skinless chicken tenders
- ¼ cup hot sauce
- 1 ½ ounces pork rinds, finely ground
- 1 teaspoon chili powder
- 1 teaspoon garlic powder

Directions:

1. Put the chicken breasts in a suitable bowl and pour hot sauce over them.
2. Toss to coat. Mix ground pork rinds, chili powder and garlic powder in another bowl.
3. Place each tender in the ground pork rinds, and coat well.
4. With wet hands, press down the pork rinds into the chicken.
5. Place the tender in a single layer into the air fryer basket.
6. Cook at almost 375 degrees F/ 190 degrees C for 20 minutes. Flip once at the middle of cooking time.
7. Serve.

French Mustard Chicken Thighs

Servings: 4
Cooking Time: 15 Minutes

Ingredients:

- 1-pound bone-in or boneless, skinless chicken thighs
- Black pepper and salt to taste
- 2 garlic cloves, minced
- ½ cup honey
- ¼ cup French mustard
- 2 tablespoons butter
- 2 tablespoon dill, chopped
- Herbs de Provence seasoning, as needed

Directions:

1. At 390 degrees F/ 200 degrees C, preheat your Air fryer.
2. Grease its air fryer basket with cooking spray.
3. In a suitable bowl, mix the Herbs de Provence seasoning, salt, and black pepper. Rub the chicken with this mixture.
4. Transfer to the cooking basket.
5. Cook for almost 15 minutes, flipping once halfway through.
6. Meanwhile, melt the butter in a suitable saucepan over medium heat.
7. Add honey, French mustard, and garlic; cook until reduced to a thick consistency, about 3 minutes.
8. Serve the chicken drizzled with the honey-mustard sauce.

Spiced Chicken With Pork Rind

Servings: 6
Cooking Time: 12 Minutes

Ingredients:

- 4 eggs
- 1 ½ pounds chicken breasts, diced into small chunks
- 1 teaspoon paprika
- ½ teaspoon garlic powder
- 1 teaspoon onion powder
- 2 ½ cups pork rind, crushed
- ¼ cup coconut flour
- Black pepper
- Salt

Directions:

1. In a suitable bowl, mix together coconut flour, black pepper, and salt.
2. In another bowl, whisk eggs until combined.
3. Take 1 more bowl and mix together pork panko, paprika, garlic powder, and onion powder.
4. Add chicken pieces in a suitable mixing bowl. Sprinkle coconut flour mixture over chicken and toss well.
5. Dip chicken pieces in the prepared egg mixture and coat with pork panko mixture and place on a plate.
6. Grease its air fryer basket with cooking spray.
7. At 400 degrees F/ 205 degrees C, preheat your Air fryer.
8. Add ½ prepared chicken in air fryer basket and cook for almost 10-12 minutes. Shake basket halfway through.
9. Cook remaining ½ using the same method.
10. Serve and enjoy.

Crispy Chicken Cordon Bleu

Servings: 4
Cooking Time: 13 To 15 Minutes

Ingredients:

- 4 chicken breast fillets
- ¼ cup chopped ham
- ⅓ cup grated Swiss or Gruyère cheese
- ¼ cup flour
- Pinch salt
- Freshly ground black pepper, to taste
- ½ teaspoon dried marjoram
- 1 egg
- 1 cup panko bread crumbs
- Olive oil for misting

Directions:

1. Preheat the air fryer to 380ºF (193ºC).
2. Put the chicken breast fillets on a work surface and gently press them with the palm of your hand to make them a bit thinner. Don't tear the meat.
3. In a small bowl, combine the ham and cheese. Divide this mixture among the chicken fillets. Wrap the chicken around the filling to enclose it, using toothpicks to hold the chicken together.
4. In a shallow bowl, mix the flour, salt, pepper, and marjoram. In another bowl, beat the egg. Spread the bread crumbs out on a plate.
5. Dip the chicken into the flour mixture, then into the egg, then into the bread crumbs to coat thoroughly.
6. Put the chicken in the air fryer basket and mist with olive oil.
7. Bake for 13 to 15 minutes or until the chicken is thoroughly cooked to 165ºF (74ºC). Carefully remove the toothpicks and serve.

Tender Chicken With Parmesan Cheese

Servings: 2
Cooking Time: 20 Minutes

Ingredients:

- 1 tablespoon butter, melted
- 2 chicken breasts
- 2 tablespoons parmesan cheese
- 6 tablespoons almond flour

Directions:

1. At 350 degrees F/ 175 degrees C, preheat your Air Fryer.
2. Combine the 6 tablespoons of almond flour and parmesan cheese in a plate.
3. Drizzle the chicken breasts with butter.
4. Dredge in the almond flour mixture.
5. Place in the air fryer basket.
6. Cook for 20 minutes at 350 degrees F/ 175 degrees C.
7. When cooked, serve and enjoy.

Cilantro-lime Chicken

Servings: 4
Cooking Time: 20 Minutes
Ingredients:
- 4 (4-ounce) boneless, skinless chicken breasts
- Chicken seasoning or rub
- Salt
- Pepper
- ½ cup chopped fresh cilantro
- Juice of 1 lime
- Cooking oil

Directions:
1. Season the chicken with the chicken seasoning, salt, and pepper to taste.
2. Place the chicken in a sealable plastic bag. Add the cilantro and lime juice.
3. Marinate the chicken in the refrigerator for 30 minutes or up to 8 hours.
4. When ready to cook, spray the air fryer basket with cooking oil.
5. Place the chicken in the air fryer. Do not stack. Cook in batches. Spray the chicken with cooking oil. Cook for 7 minutes.
6. Open the air fryer and flip the chicken. Cook for an additional 3 minutes.
7. Remove the cooked chicken from the air fryer, then repeat steps 5 and 6 for the remaining chicken breasts.
8. Cool before serving.

Tandoori Chicken

Servings: 4
Cooking Time:18 To 23 Minutes
Ingredients:
- ⅔ cup plain low-fat yogurt
- 2 tablespoons freshly squeezed lemon juice
- 2 teaspoons curry powder (see Tip)
- ½ teaspoon ground cinnamon
- 2 garlic cloves, minced
- 2 teaspoons olive oil
- 4 (5-ounce) low-sodium boneless skinless chicken breasts

Directions:
1. In a medium bowl, whisk the yogurt, lemon juice, curry powder, cinnamon, garlic, and olive oil.
2. With a sharp knife, cut thin slashes into the chicken. Add it to the yogurt mixture and turn to coat. Let stand for 10 minutes at room temperature. You can also prepare this ahead of time and marinate the chicken in the refrigerator for up to 24 hours.
3. Remove the chicken from the marinade and shake off any excess liquid. Discard any remaining marinade.
4. Roast the chicken for 10 minutes. With tongs, carefully turn each piece. Roast for 8 to 13 minutes more, or until the chicken reaches an internal temperature of 165°F on a meat thermometer. Serve immediately.

Roasted Veggie Chicken Salad

Servings: 4
Cooking Time: 10 To 13 Minutes

Ingredients:
- 3 boneless, skinless chicken breasts, cut into 1-inch cubes
- 1 small red onion, sliced
- 1 orange bell pepper, sliced
- 1 cup sliced yellow summer squash
- 4 tablespoons honey mustard salad dressing, divided
- ½ teaspoon dried thyme
- ½ cup mayonnaise
- 2 tablespoons lemon juice

Directions:
1. Place the chicken, onion, pepper, and squash in the air fryer basket. Drizzle with 1 tablespoon of the honey mustard salad dressing, add the thyme, and toss.
2. Roast for 10 to 13 minutes or until the chicken is 165°F on a food thermometer, tossing the food once during cooking time.
3. Transfer the chicken and vegetables to a bowl and mix in the remaining 3 tablespoons of honey mustard salad dressing, the mayonnaise, and lemon juice. Serve on lettuce leaves, if desired.

Garlic-roasted Chicken With Creamer Potatoes

Servings: 4
Cooking Time: 25 Minutes

Ingredients:
- 1 (2½- to 3-pound) broiler-fryer whole chicken
- 2 tablespoons olive oil
- ½ teaspoon garlic salt
- 8 cloves garlic, peeled
- 1 slice lemon
- ½ teaspoon dried thyme
- ½ teaspoon dried marjoram
- 12 to 16 creamer potatoes, scrubbed

Directions:
1. Do not wash the chicken before cooking. Remove it from its packaging and pat the chicken dry.
2. Combine the olive oil and salt in a small bowl. Rub half of this mixture on the inside of the chicken, under the skin, and on the chicken skin. Place the garlic cloves and lemon slice inside the chicken. Sprinkle the chicken with the thyme and marjoram.
3. Put the chicken in the air fryer basket. Surround with the potatoes and drizzle the potatoes with the remaining olive oil mixture.
4. Roast for 25 minutes, then test the temperature of the chicken. It should be 160°F. Test at the thickest part of the breast, making sure the probe doesn't touch bone. If the chicken isn't done yet, return it to the air fryer and roast it for 4 to 5 minutes, or until the temperature is 160°F.
5. When the chicken is done, transfer it and the potatoes to a serving platter and cover with foil. Let the chicken rest for 5 minutes before serving.

Crisp Paprika Chicken Drumsticks

Servings: 2
Cooking Time: 22 Minutes

Ingredients:

- 2 teaspoons paprika
- 1 teaspoon packed brown sugar
- 1 teaspoon garlic powder
- ½ teaspoon dry mustard
- ½ teaspoon salt
- Pinch pepper
- 4 (5-ounce / 142-g) chicken drumsticks, trimmed
- 1 teaspoon vegetable oil
- 1 scallion, green part only, sliced thin on bias

Directions:

1. Preheat the air fryer to 400°F (204°C).
2. Combine paprika, sugar, garlic powder, mustard, salt, and pepper in a bowl. Pat drumsticks dry with paper towels. Using metal skewer, poke 10 to 15 holes in skin of each drumstick. Rub with oil and sprinkle evenly with spice mixture.
3. Arrange drumsticks in air fryer basket, spaced evenly apart, alternating ends. Air fry until chicken is crisp and registers 195°F (91°C), 22 to 25 minutes, flipping chicken halfway through cooking.
4. Transfer chicken to serving platter, tent loosely with aluminum foil, and let rest for 5 minutes. Sprinkle with scallion and serve.

Pecan-crusted Turkey Cutlets

Servings: 4
Cooking Time: 10 To 12 Minutes

Ingredients:

- ¾ cup panko bread crumbs
- ¼ teaspoon salt
- ¼ teaspoon pepper
- ¼ teaspoon dry mustard
- ¼ teaspoon poultry seasoning
- ½ cup pecans
- ¼ cup cornstarch
- 1 egg, beaten
- 1 pound (454 g) turkey cutlets, ½-inch thick
- Salt and pepper, to taste
- Cooking spray

Directions:

1. Preheat the air fryer to 360°F (182°C).
2. Place the panko crumbs, salt, pepper, mustard, and poultry seasoning in a food processor. Process until crumbs are finely crushed. Add pecans and process just until nuts are finely chopped.
3. Place cornstarch in a shallow dish and beaten egg in another. Transfer coating mixture from food processor into a third shallow dish.
4. Sprinkle turkey cutlets with salt and pepper to taste.
5. Dip cutlets in cornstarch and shake off excess, then dip in beaten egg and finally roll in crumbs, pressing to coat well. Spray both sides with cooking spray.
6. Place 2 cutlets in air fryer basket in a single layer and air fry for 10 to 12 minutes. Repeat with the remaining cutlets.
7. Serve warm.

Parmesan Chicken Tenderloins

Servings: 6
Cooking Time: 12 Minutes
Ingredients:

- 1 lime
- 2 pounds' chicken tenderloins, cut up
- ½ cup pork rinds, crushed
- ½ cup Parmesan cheese, grated
- 1 tablespoon olive oil
- Salt and black pepper, to taste
- 1 teaspoon cayenne pepper
- ⅓ teaspoon ground cumin
- 1 teaspoon chili powder
- 1 egg

Directions:
1. Squeeze and rub the lime juice all over the chicken.
2. Spritz the cooking basket with a nonstick cooking spray.
3. In a suitable mixing bowl, thoroughly combine the pork rinds, Parmesan, olive oil, salt, black pepper, cayenne pepper, cumin, and chili powder.
4. In a suitable shallow bowl, whisk the egg until well beaten.
5. Dip the chicken tenders in the egg, then in pork rind mixture.
6. Transfer the coated and breaded chicken to the prepared cooking basket.
7. Cook in the preheated Air Fryer at 380 degrees F/ 195 degrees C for 12 minutes almost.
8. Turn them once cooked halfway through.
9. Serve immediately.

Lemon Parmesan Chicken

Servings: 4
Cooking Time: 20 Minutes
Ingredients:

- 1 egg
- 2 tablespoons lemon juice
- 2 teaspoons minced garlic
- ½ teaspoon salt
- ½ teaspoon freshly ground black pepper
- 4 boneless, skinless chicken breasts, thin cut
- Olive oil spray
- ½ cup whole-wheat bread crumbs
- ¼ cup grated Parmesan cheese

Directions:
1. In a medium bowl, whisk together the egg, lemon juice, garlic, salt, and pepper. Add the chicken breasts, cover, and refrigerate for up to 1 hour.
2. In a shallow bowl, combine the bread crumbs and Parmesan cheese.
3. Preheat the air fryer to 360°F (182°C). Spray the air fryer basket lightly with olive oil spray.
4. Remove the chicken breasts from the egg mixture, then dredge them in the bread crumb mixture, and place in the air fryer basket in a single layer. Lightly spray the chicken breasts with olive oil spray. You may need to cook the chicken in batches.
5. Air fry for 8 minutes. Flip the chicken over, lightly spray with olive oil spray, and air fry until the chicken reaches an internal temperature of 165°F (74°C), for an additional 7 to 12 minutes.
6. Serve warm.

Indian-style Chicken With Raita

Servings: 2
Cooking Time: 12 Minutes
Ingredients:

- 2 chicken fillets
- Sea salt and ground black pepper, to taste
- 2 teaspoons garam masala
- 1 teaspoon ground turmeric
- ½ cup plain yogurt
- 1 English cucumber, shredded and drained
- 1 tablespoon fresh cilantro, coarsely chopped
- ½ red onion, chopped
- A pinch of grated nutmeg
- A pinch of ground cinnamon

Directions:
1. Before cooking, heat your air fryer to 380 degrees F/ 195 degrees C.
2. Rub pepper, garam masala, ground turmeric, and salt over the chicken fillets until well coated.
3. Cook in your air fryer for 12 minutes. Flip once or twice halfway through cooking.
4. To make additional raita, mix all the rest of the ingredients in a mixing bowl.
5. Serve the chicken with raita sauce.

Lemon-pepper Chicken Wings

Servings: 4
Cooking Time: 20 Minute
Ingredients:

- 8 whole chicken wings
- Juice of ½ lemon
- ½ teaspoon garlic powder
- 1 teaspoon onion powder
- Salt
- Pepper
- ¼ cup low-fat buttermilk
- ½ cup all-purpose flour
- Cooking oil

Directions:
1. Place the wings in a sealable plastic bag. Drizzle the wings with the lemon juice. Season the wings with the garlic powder, onion powder, and salt and pepper to taste.
2. Seal the bag. Shake thoroughly to combine the seasonings and coat the wings.
3. Pour the buttermilk and the flour into separate bowls large enough to dip the wings.
4. Spray the air fryer basket with cooking oil.
5. One at a time, dip the wings in the buttermilk and then the flour.
6. Place the wings in the air fryer basket. It is okay to stack them on top of each other. Spray the wings with cooking oil, being sure to spray the bottom layer. Cook for 5 minutes.
7. Remove the basket and shake it to ensure all of the pieces will cook fully.
8. Return the basket to the air fryer and continue to cook the chicken. Repeat shaking every 5 minutes until a total of 20 minutes has passed.
9. Cool before serving.

Cajun Chicken Drumsticks

Servings: 5
Cooking Time: 40 Minutes
Ingredients:
- 10 chicken drumsticks
- 1½ tablespoons Louisiana Cajun Seasoning
- Salt
- Pepper
- Cooking oil

Directions:
1. Season the drumsticks with the Cajun seasoning and salt and pepper to taste.
2. Spray the air fryer basket with cooking oil.
3. Place 5 drumsticks in the air fryer. Do not stack. Spray the drumsticks with cooking oil. Cook for 10 minutes.
4. Open the air fryer and flip the chicken. Cook for an additional 8 minutes.
5. Remove the cooked chicken from the air fryer, then repeat steps 3 and 4 for the remaining 5 drumsticks.
6. Cool before serving.

Chicken Wings With Lemon Pepper

Servings: 4
Cooking Time: 16 Minutes
Ingredients:
- 1-pound chicken wings
- 1 teaspoon lemon pepper
- 1 tablespoon olive oil
- 1 teaspoon salt

Directions:
1. Add chicken wings into the suitable mixing bowl.
2. Add the remaining ingredients over chicken and toss well to coat.
3. Place chicken wings in the air fryer basket.
4. Cook chicken wings for 8 minutes at 400 degrees F/ 205 degrees C.
5. Turn chicken wings to another side and cook for 8 minutes more.
6. Serve and enjoy.

Turkey And Cranberry Quesadillas

Servings: 4
Cooking Time: 4 To 8 Minutes

Ingredients:

- 6 low-sodium whole-wheat tortillas
- ⅓ cup shredded low-sodium low-fat Swiss cheese
- ¾ cup shredded cooked low-sodium turkey breast
- 2 tablespoons cranberry sauce
- 2 tablespoons dried cranberries
- ½ teaspoon dried basil
- Olive oil spray, for spraying the tortillas

Directions:

1. Preheat the air fryer to 400°F (204°C).
2. Put 3 tortillas on a work surface.
3. Evenly divide the Swiss cheese, turkey, cranberry sauce, and dried cranberries among the tortillas. Sprinkle with the basil and top with the remaining tortillas.
4. Spray the outsides of the tortillas with olive oil spray.
5. One at a time, air fry the quesadillas in the air fryer for 4 to 8 minutes, or until crisp and the cheese is melted. Cut into quarters and serve.

Roasted Turkey With Veggies

Servings: 4
Cooking Time: 1 Hour 15 Minutes

Ingredients:

- 1 red onion, cut into wedges
- 1 carrot, trimmed and sliced
- 1 celery stalk, trimmed and sliced
- 1 cup Brussel sprouts, trimmed and halved
- 1 cup roasted vegetable broth
- 1 tablespoon. apple cider vinegar
- 1 teaspoon. maple syrup
- 2 turkey thighs
- ½ teaspoon. mixed peppercorns, freshly cracked
- 1 teaspoon fine sea salt
- 1 teaspoon cayenne pepper
- 1 teaspoon onion powder
- ½ teaspoon garlic powder
- ⅓ teaspoon mustard seeds

Directions:

1. Arrange the veggies on a baking dish that fits in your air fryer.
2. Pour roasted vegetable broth in the dish.
3. Place the remaining ingredients in a large-sized bowl. Then set it aside to marinate for about 30 minutes.
4. Then add over the veggies.
5. Roast in your air fryer at 330 degrees F/ 165 degrees C for 40 to 45 minutes.
6. Serve and enjoy!

Beef, Pork & Lamb Recipes

Marinated Pork Tenderloin

Servings: 6
Cooking Time: 30 Minutes

Ingredients:
- ¼ cup olive oil
- ¼ cup soy sauce
- ¼ cup freshly squeezed lemon juice
- 1 garlic clove, minced
- 1 tablespoon Dijon mustard
- 1 teaspoon salt
- ½ teaspoon freshly ground black pepper
- 2 pounds (907 g) pork tenderloin

Directions:
1. In a large mixing bowl, make the marinade: Mix the olive oil, soy sauce, lemon juice, minced garlic, Dijon mustard, salt, and pepper. Reserve ¼ cup of the marinade.
2. Put the tenderloin in a large bowl and pour the remaining marinade over the meat. Cover and marinate in the refrigerator for about 1 hour.
3. Preheat the air fryer to 400ºF (204ºC).
4. Put the marinated pork tenderloin into the air fryer basket. Roast for 10 minutes. Flip the pork and baste it with half of the reserved marinade. Roast for 10 minutes more.
5. Flip the pork, then baste with the remaining marinade. Roast for another 10 minutes, for a total cooking time of 30 minutes.
6. Serve immediately.

Garlic Steak With Cheese Butter

Servings: 2
Cooking Time: 10 Minutes

Ingredients:
- 2 rib-eye steaks
- 2 teaspoons garlic powder
- 2 ½ tablespoons blue cheese butter
- 1 teaspoon black pepper
- 2 teaspoons kosher salt

Directions:
1. At 400 degrees F/ 205 degrees C, preheat your air fryer.
2. Mix together garlic powder, black pepper, and salt and rub over the steaks.
3. Grease its air fryer basket with cooking spray.
4. Place trimmed steak in the air fryer basket and cook for 4 -5 minutes on each side.
5. Top with blue butter cheese.
6. Serve and enjoy.

Beef And Pork Sausage Meatloaf

Servings: 4
Cooking Time: 25 Minutes
Ingredients:
- ¾ pound (340 g) ground chuck
- 4 ounces (113 g) ground pork sausage
- 1 cup shallots, finely chopped
- 2 eggs, well beaten
- 3 tablespoons plain milk
- 1 tablespoon oyster sauce
- 1 teaspoon porcini mushrooms
- ½ teaspoon cumin powder
- 1 teaspoon garlic paste
- 1 tablespoon fresh parsley
- Salt and crushed red pepper flakes, to taste
- 1 cup crushed saltines
- Cooking spray

Directions:
1. Preheat the air fryer to 360°F (182°C). Sprtiz a baking dish with cooking spray.
2. Mix all the ingredients in a large bowl, combining everything well.
3. Transfer to the baking dish and bake in the air fryer for 25 minutes.
4. Serve hot.

Garlic Lamb Rack

Servings: 6
Cooking Time: 30 Minutes
Ingredients:
- 1 egg, lightly beaten
- ½ tablespoon fresh thyme, chopped
- 1 ¾ lbs. rack of lamb
- ½ tablespoon fresh rosemary, chopped
- 1 tablespoon olive oil
- 2 garlic cloves, chopped
- Pepper
- Salt

Directions:
1. Mix up the oil and garlic, then brush the lamb rack with the mixture.
2. Season the lamb rack with pepper and salt.
3. After mix the thyme and rosemary well, coat the lamb rack with the egg and the herb mixture.
4. Place lamb rack in the air fryer basket and cook for at 390 degrees F/ 200 degrees C for 30 minutes.
5. After 25 minutes of cooking time, turn the lamb rack and cook for 5 minutes more.
6. Serve and enjoy.

Classic Spring Rolls

Servings: 20
Cooking Time: 8 Minutes

Ingredients:

- ⅓ cup noodles
- 1 cup ground beef
- 1 teaspoon soy sauce
- 1 cup fresh mix vegetables
- 3 garlic cloves, minced
- 1 small onion, diced
- 1 tablespoon sesame oil
- 1 packet spring roll sheets
- 2 tablespoons cold water

Directions:

1. Cook the noodle in enough hot water to soften them up, drain them and snip them to make them shorter.
2. In a frying pan over medium heat, cook the beef, soy sauce, mixed vegetables, garlic, and onion in sesame oil until the beef is cooked through. Take the pan off the heat and throw in the noodles. Mix well to incorporate everything.
3. Unroll a spring roll sheet and lay it flat. Scatter the filling diagonally across it and roll it up, brushing the edges lightly with water to act as an adhesive. Repeat until you have used up all the sheets and the filling.
4. Preheat the air fryer to 350°F (177°C).
5. Coat each spring roll with a light brushing of oil and transfer to the air fryer.
6. Air fry for 8 minutes and serve hot.

Elegant Pork Chops

Servings: 4
Cooking Time: 25 Minutes

Ingredients:

- 4 pork chops, bone-in
- Salt and black pepper, to taste
- ½ teaspoon onion powder
- ½ teaspoon paprika
- ½ teaspoon celery seeds
- 2 cooking apples, peeled and sliced
- 1 tablespoon honey
- 1 tablespoon peanut oil

Directions:

1. Place the pork in a suitable greased baking pan.
2. Season with black pepper and salt, and transfer the pan to the cooking basket.
3. Cook the pork chops in the preheated air fryer at about 370 degrees F/ 185 degrees C for almost 10 minutes.
4. Meanwhile, in a suitable saucepan, simmer the remaining ingredients over medium heat for about 8 minutes or until the apples are softened.
5. Pour the applesauce over the prepared pork chops.
6. Add to the preheated Air Fryer and air fry for 5 minutes more.
7. Serve

Pork Chops With Sage Leaves

Servings: 4
Cooking Time: 25 Minutes

Ingredients:
- ¼ teaspoon black pepper
- 4 cups stuffing mix
- ½ teaspoon salt
- 2 tablespoons olive oil
- 4 garlic cloves, minced
- 2 tablespoons sage leaves

Directions:
1. At 350 degrees F/ 175 degrees C, preheat your air fryer.
2. Cut a hole in pork chops and fill chops with stuffing mix.
3. In a suitable bowl, mix sage leaves, garlic cloves, oil, black pepper and salt.
4. Cover chops with marinade and let marinate for almost 10 minutes.
5. Place the chops in your air fryer basket and cook for 25 minutes.
6. Serve and enjoy!

Crispy Mustard Pork Tenderloin

Servings:4
Cooking Time: 14 Minutes

Ingredients:
- 1 pound pork tenderloin, cut into 1-inch slices
- Pinch salt
- Freshly ground black pepper
- 2 tablespoons Dijon mustard
- 1 clove garlic, minced
- ½ teaspoon dried basil
- 1 cup soft bread crumbs
- 2 tablespoons olive oil

Directions:
1. Slightly pound the pork slices until they are about ¾-inch thick. Sprinkle with salt and pepper on both sides.
2. Coat the pork with the Dijon mustard and sprinkle with the garlic and basil.
3. On a plate, combine the bread crumbs and olive oil and mix well. Coat the pork slices with the bread crumb mixture, patting so the crumbs adhere.
4. Place the pork in the air fryer basket, leaving a little space between each piece. Air-fry for 12 to 14 minutes or until the pork reaches at least 145°F on a meat thermometer and the coating is crisp and brown. Serve immediately.

Spiced Pork Chops

Servings: 2
Cooking Time: 20 Minutes
Ingredients:
- 1 tablespoon olive oil
- ½ lb. pork chops
- ½ teaspoon dried oregano
- ¼ teaspoon red pepper flakes
- 1 teaspoon dried thyme
- ½ teaspoon salt
- ½ teaspoon pepper
- 6 large mushrooms, cleaned and sliced
- 1 large yellow onion, chopped
- 1 ½ tablespoons soy sauce
- 2 tablespoons fresh parsley, finely chopped

Directions:
1. Mix the pork chops with the onion, mushrooms, pepper, red pepper flakes, thyme, oregano, olive oil, soy sauce, and olive oil in a large bowl.
2. When coated, cook the pork chops and clean mushrooms in your air fryer at 390 degrees F/ 200 degrees C for 20 minutes.
3. Sprinkle with the fresh parsley, serve and enjoy!

Carne Asada Tacos

Servings: 4
Cooking Time: 14 Minutes
Ingredients:
- ⅓ cup olive oil
- 1½ pounds (680 g) flank steak
- Salt and freshly ground black pepper, to taste
- ⅓ cup freshly squeezed lime juice
- ½ cup chopped fresh cilantro
- 4 teaspoons minced garlic
- 1 teaspoon ground cumin
- 1 teaspoon chili powder

Directions:
1. Brush the air fryer basket with olive oil.
2. Put the flank steak in a large mixing bowl. Season with salt and pepper.
3. Add the lime juice, cilantro, garlic, cumin, and chili powder and toss to coat the steak.
4. For the best flavor, let the steak marinate in the refrigerator for about 1 hour.
5. Preheat the air fryer to 400°F (204°C)
6. Put the steak in the air fryer basket. Air fry for 7 minutes. Flip the steak. Air fry for 7 minutes more or until an internal temperature reaches at least 145°F (63°C).
7. Let the steak rest for about 5 minutes, then cut into strips to serve.

Air Fried Lamb Ribs

Servings: 4
Cooking Time: 18 Minutes
Ingredients:

- 2 tablespoons mustard
- 1 pound (454 g) lamb ribs
- 1 teaspoon rosemary, chopped
- Salt and ground black pepper, to taste
- ¼ cup mint leaves, chopped
- 1 cup Green yogurt

Directions:

1. Preheat the air fryer to 350°F (177°C).
2. Use a brush to apply the mustard to the lamb ribs, and season with rosemary, salt, and pepper.
3. Air fry the ribs in the air fryer for 18 minutes.
4. Meanwhile, combine the mint leaves and yogurt in a bowl.
5. Remove the lamb ribs from the air fryer when cooked and serve with the mint yogurt.

Super Bacon With Meat

Servings: 4
Cooking Time: 1 Hour
Ingredients:

- 30 slices thick-cut bacon
- 4 ounces (113 g) Cheddar cheese, shredded
- 12 ounces (340 g) steak
- 10 ounces (283 g) pork sausage
- Salt and ground black pepper, to taste

Directions:

1. Preheat the air fryer to 400°F (204°C).
2. Lay out 30 slices of bacon in a woven pattern and bake for 20 minutes until crisp. Put the cheese in the center of the bacon.
3. Combine the steak and sausage to form a meaty mixture.
4. Lay out the meat in a rectangle of similar size to the bacon strips. Season with salt and pepper.
5. Roll the meat into a tight roll and refrigerate.
6. Preheat the air fryer to 400°F (204°C).
7. Make a 7×7 bacon weave and roll the bacon weave over the meat, diagonally.
8. Bake for 60 minutes or until the internal temperature reaches at least 165°F (74°C).
9. Let rest for 5 minutes before serving.

Ham And Cheese Stromboli

Servings: 6
Cooking Time: 20 Minutes
Ingredients:
- 1 teaspoon all-purpose flour
- 1 (13-ounce) can refrigerated pizza dough
- 6 slices provolone cheese
- ½ cup shredded mozzarella cheese
- 12 slices deli ham
- ½ red bell pepper, seeded and sliced
- ½ teaspoon dried basil
- ½ teaspoon oregano
- Pepper
- Cooking oil

Directions:
1. Sprinkle the flour on a flat work surface. Roll out the pizza dough. Cut the dough into 6 equal-sized rectangles.
2. Add 1 slice of provolone, 1 tablespoon of mozzarella, 2 slices of ham, and a few slices of red bell pepper to each of the rectangles.
3. Season each with dried basil, oregano, and pepper to taste.
4. Fold up each crust to close the stromboli. Using the back of a fork, press along the open edges to seal.
5. Place the stromboli in the air fryer. Do not stack. Cook in batches. Spray the stromboli with cooking oil. Cook for 10 minutes.
6. Remove the cooked stromboli from the air fryer, then repeat step 5 for the remaining stromboli.
7. Cool before serving.

Delicious Cheeseburger

Servings: 2
Cooking Time: 12 Minutes
Ingredients:
- ½ pound ground beef
- ¼ teaspoon onion powder
- 2 cheese slices
- ¼ teaspoon black pepper
- ⅛ teaspoon salt

Directions:
1. In a suitable bowl, mix together ground beef, onion powder, black pepper, and salt.
2. Make 2 equal shapes of patties from meat mixture and place in the air fryer basket.
3. Cook patties at 370 degrees F/ 185 degrees C for 12 minutes. Turn patties halfway through.
4. Once air fryer timer goes off then place cheese slices on top of each patty and close the air fryer basket for 1 minute.
5. Serve and enjoy.

Pork Chops With Rinds

Servings: 4
Cooking Time: 15 Minutes
Ingredients:
- 1 teaspoon chili powder
- ½ teaspoon garlic powder
- 1½ ounces (43 g) pork rinds, finely ground
- 4 (4-ounce / 113-g) pork chops
- 1 tablespoon coconut oil, melted

Directions:
1. Preheat the air fryer to 400°F (204°C).
2. Combine the chili powder, garlic powder, and ground pork rinds.
3. Coat the pork chops with the coconut oil, followed by the pork rind mixture, taking care to cover them completely. Then place the chops in the air fryer basket.
4. Air fry the chops for 15 minutes or until the internal temperature of the chops reaches at least 145°F (63°C), turning halfway through.
5. Serve immediately.

Spiced Rib Eye Steak

Servings: 3
Cooking Time: 9 Minutes
Ingredients:
- 1 lb. rib eye steak
- ½-teaspoon chipotle powder
- ¼-teaspoon paprika
- ¼-teaspoon onion powder
- ½-teaspoon garlic powder
- ½ teaspoon chili powder
- ¼-teaspoon black pepper
- ⅛ teaspoon coffee powder
- ⅛-teaspoon cocoa powder
- ⅛-teaspoon coriander powder
- 1 ½-teaspoon sea salt

Directions:
1. In addition to the steak, mix the other ingredients well in a small bowl.
2. Rub the steak with the spice mixture and marinate the steak for 20 minutes.
3. Coat the cooking basket of your air fryer with cooking spray.
4. Cook the marinated steak on the basket in your air fryer at 390 degrees F/ 200 degrees C for 9 minutes.
5. Once done, serve and enjoy.

Bacon And Pear Stuffed Pork Chops

Servings: 3
Cooking Time: 24 Minutes

Ingredients:
- 4 slices bacon, chopped
- 1 tablespoon butter
- ½ cup finely diced onion
- ⅓ cup chicken stock
- 1½ cups seasoned stuffing cubes
- 1 egg, beaten
- ½ teaspoon dried thyme
- ½ teaspoon salt
- ⅛ teaspoon freshly ground black pepper
- 1 pear, finely diced
- ⅓ cup crumbled blue cheese
- 3 boneless center-cut pork chops (2-inch thick)
- Olive oil, for greasing
- Salt and freshly ground black pepper, to taste

Directions:
1. Preheat the air fryer to 400°F (204°C).
2. Put the bacon into the air fryer basket and air fry for 6 minutes, stirring halfway through the cooking time. Remove the bacon and set it aside on a paper towel. Pour out the grease from the bottom of the air fryer.
3. To make the stuffing, melt the butter in a medium saucepan over medium heat on the stovetop. Add the onion and sauté for a few minutes until it starts to soften. Add the chicken stock and simmer for 1 minute. Remove the pan from the heat and add the stuffing cubes. Stir until the stock has been absorbed. Add the egg, dried thyme, salt and freshly ground black pepper, and stir until combined. Fold in the diced pear and crumbled blue cheese.
4. Put the pork chops on a cutting board. Using the palm of the hand to hold the chop flat and steady, slice into the side of the pork chop to make a pocket in the center of the chop. Leave about an inch of chop uncut and make sure you don't cut all the way through the pork chop. Brush both sides of the pork chops with olive oil and season with salt and freshly ground black pepper. Stuff each pork chop with a third of the stuffing, packing the stuffing tightly inside the pocket.
5. Preheat the air fryer to 360°F (182°C).
6. Spray or brush the sides of the air fryer basket with oil. Put the pork chops in the air fryer basket with the open, stuffed edge of the pork chop facing the outside edges of the basket.
7. Air fry the pork chops for 18 minutes, turning the pork chops over halfway through the cooking time. When the chops are done, let them rest for 5 minutes and then transfer to a serving platter.

Crumbed Golden Filet Mignon

Servings: 4
Cooking Time: 12 Minutes

Ingredients:

- ½ pound (227 g) filet mignon
- Sea salt and ground black pepper, to taste
- ½ teaspoon cayenne pepper
- 1 teaspoon dried basil
- 1 teaspoon dried rosemary
- 1 teaspoon dried thyme
- 1 tablespoon sesame oil
- 1 small egg, whisked
- ½ cup bread crumbs

Directions:

1. Preheat the air fryer to 360°F (182°C).
2. Cover the filet mignon with the salt, black pepper, cayenne pepper, basil, rosemary, and thyme. Coat with sesame oil.
3. Put the egg in a shallow plate.
4. Pour the bread crumbs in another plate.
5. Dip the filet mignon into the egg. Roll it into the crumbs.
6. Transfer the steak to the air fryer and air fry for 12 minutes or until it turns golden.
7. Serve immediately.

Italian-style Honey Pork

Servings: 3
Cooking Time: 50 Minutes

Ingredients:

- 1 teaspoon Celtic sea salt
- ½-teaspoon black pepper, freshly cracked
- ¼ cup red wine
- 1 tablespoon mustard
- 1 tablespoon honey
- 2 garlic cloves, minced
- 1 lb. pork top loin
- 1 tablespoon Italian herb seasoning blend

Directions:

1. Prepare a suitable bowl, mix up the salt, black pepper, red wine, mustard, honey, garlic and the pork top loin, then marinate the pork top loin at least 30 minutes.
2. Spray the cooking basket of your air fryer with the non-stick cooking spray.
3. Sprinkle the Italian herb on the top of the pork top loin after transfer it to the basket.
4. Cook the pork top loin at 370 degrees F/ 185 degrees C for 10 minutes, flipping and spraying with cooking oil halfway through.
5. When cooked, serve and enjoy.

Juicy Cheeseburger

Servings: 4 Servings
Cooking Time: 20 Minutes

Ingredients:
- 1 pound of 80/20 ground chuck beef
- 4 buns
- 4 slices of any cheese you like
- 1 ½ tablespoons of burger seasonings
- 1 teaspoon of Worcestershire sauce
- 1 teaspoon of liquid smoke
- Lettuce leaves, slices of tomatoes, onions, ketchup, for serving
- Pinch of salt and black pepper, to taste

Directions:
1. Preheat your air fryer to 360ºF.
2. Add the ground beef, sauce, liquid smoke, seasonings, black pepper, and salt in a large mixing bowl. Mix it until smooth and make 4 patties.
3. Put the formed patties in the air fryer basket and cook at 360ºF for 8 minutes. Flip them and cook for an extra 3–4 minutes.
4. Serve on buns* with ketchup, lettuce leaves, slices of onions, and tomatoes. Enjoy your Juicy Cheeseburger!

Tender Country Ribs

Servings: 4
Cooking Time: 20 To 25 Minutes

Ingredients:
- 12 country-style pork ribs, trimmed of excess fat
- 2 tablespoons cornstarch
- 2 tablespoons olive oil
- 1 teaspoon dry mustard
- ½ teaspoon thyme
- ½ teaspoon garlic powder
- 1 teaspoon dried marjoram
- Pinch salt
- Freshly ground black pepper

Directions:
1. Place the ribs on a clean work surface.
2. In a small bowl, combine the cornstarch, olive oil, mustard, thyme, garlic powder, marjoram, salt, and pepper, and rub into the ribs.
3. Place the ribs in the air fryer basket and roast for 10 minutes.
4. Carefully turn the ribs using tongs and roast for 10 to 15 minutes or until the ribs are crisp and register an internal temperature of at least 150°F.

Stir-fried Steak And Cabbage

Servings: 4
Cooking Time: 8 To 13 Minutes

Ingredients:

- ½ pound sirloin steak, cut into strips
- 2 teaspoons cornstarch
- 1 tablespoon peanut oil
- 2 cups chopped red or green cabbage
- 1 yellow bell pepper, chopped
- 2 green onions, chopped
- 2 cloves garlic, sliced
- ½ cup commercial stir-fry sauce

Directions:

1. Toss the steak with the cornstarch and set aside.
2. In a 6-inch metal bowl, combine the peanut oil with the cabbage. Place in the basket and cook for 3 to 4 minutes.
3. Remove the bowl from the basket and add the steak, pepper, onions, and garlic. Return to the air fryer and cook for 3 to 5 minutes or until the steak is cooked to desired doneness and vegetables are crisp and tender.
4. Add the stir-fry sauce and cook for 2 to 4 minutes or until hot. Serve over rice.

Fish And Seafood Recipes

Bean Burritos With Cheddar Cheese

Servings: 4
Cooking Time: 15 Minutes

Ingredients:

- 4 tortillas
- 1 can beans
- 1 cup cheddar cheese, grated
- ¼-teaspoon paprika
- ¼-teaspoon chili powder
- ¼-teaspoon garlic powder
- Salt and pepper to taste

Directions:

1. Heat the Air Fryer to 350 degrees F/ 175 degrees C ahead of time.
2. Mix up the paprika, chili powder, garlic powder, salt and pepper in a suitable bowl.
3. Before adding the spice mixture and cheddar cheese, fill each tortilla with an equal portion of beans.
4. Roll the tortilla wraps into burritos.
5. Use the parchment paper to cover the base of a baking dish.
6. Arrange the burritos to the baking dish and place the dish in the air fryer.
7. Cook the burritos for about 5 minutes at 350 degrees F/ 175 degrees C.
8. When cooked, serve hot.

Sea Bass With Greek-style Sauce

Servings: 2
Cooking Time: 11 Minutes
Ingredients:

- ½ pound sea bass
- 1 garlic clove, halved
- Sea salt, to taste
- Ground black pepper, to taste
- ½ teaspoon rigani (Greek oregano)
- ½ teaspoon dried dill weed
- ¼ teaspoon ground bay leaf
- ¼ teaspoon ground cumin
- ½ teaspoon shallot powder
- Greek sauce:
- ½ Greek yogurt
- 1 teaspoon olive oil
- ½ teaspoon Tzatziki spice mix
- 1 teaspoon lime juice

Directions:
1. Use kitchen towels to pat dry the sea bass.
2. Use garlic halves to rub the sea bass.
3. Toss the sea bass well with rigani, dill, ground bay leaf, ground cumin, shallot powder, salt and black pepper.
4. Cook the sea bass in your Air Fryer at 400 degrees F/ 205 degrees C for 5 minutes.
5. After that, turn the filets over and cook on the other side for 5 to 6 minutes.
6. To make the Greek-style sauce, simply blend the remaining ingredients.
7. Serve the warm fish dolloped with Greek-style sauce and enjoy!

Typical Crab Cakes With Lemon Wedges

Servings: 3
Cooking Time: 10 Minutes
Ingredients:

- 1 egg, beaten
- 2 tablespoons milk
- 2 crustless bread slices
- 1 pound lump crabmeat
- 2 tablespoons scallions, chopped
- 1 garlic clove, minced
- 1 teaspoon deli mustard
- 1 teaspoon Sriracha sauce
- Sea salt, to taste
- Ground black pepper, to taste
- 4 lemon wedges, for serving

Directions:
1. Beat the egg and milk until white and frothy, then add the bread in and let it soak for a few minutes.
2. In addition to the lemon wedges, stir in the remaining ingredients.
3. Form 4 equal-size patties, place the patties in the cooking basket of your air fryer and then spray them with a non-stick cooking spray.
4. Arrange the basket to the air fryer and cook the patties at 400 degrees F/ 205 degrees C for 10 minutes, flipping halfway through.
5. Serve warm, garnished with lemon wedges. Bon appétit!

Buttered Shrimp Fry

Servings: 4
Cooking Time: 15 Minutes

Ingredients:

- 1 tablespoon chopped chives or 1-teaspoon dried chives
- 1 tablespoon lemon juice
- 1 tablespoon basil leaves, minced, or 1 teaspoon dried basil, plus more for sprinkling
- 1 tablespoon minced garlic
- 21-25 count defrosted shrimp
- 1 tablespoon chicken stock (or white wine)
- 1 teaspoon red pepper flakes
- 1 tablespoon butter

Directions:
1. Lightly spray the baking pan of your air fryer.
2. Melt butter for 2 minutes at 330 degrees F/ 165 degrees C.
3. After stirring in red pepper flakes and garlic, cook for 3 minutes.
4. Add remaining ingredients in pan and toss well to coat.
5. Cook for 5 minutes at 330 degrees F/ 165 degrees C.
6. Stir and let it stand for another 5 minutes.
7. When done, serve and enjoy.

Beer-battered Fish And Chips

Servings: 4
Cooking Time: 30 Minutes

Ingredients:

- 2 eggs
- 1 cup malty beer, such as Pabst Blue Ribbon
- 1 cup all-purpose flour
- ½ cup cornstarch
- 1 teaspoon garlic powder
- Salt
- Pepper
- Cooking oil
- 4 (4-ounce) cod fillets

Directions:
1. In a medium bowl, beat the eggs with the beer. In another medium bowl, combine the flour and cornstarch, and season with the garlic powder and salt and pepper to taste.
2. Spray the air fryer basket with cooking oil.
3. Dip each cod fillet in the flour and cornstarch mixture and then in the egg and beer mixture. Dip the cod in the flour and cornstarch a second time.
4. Place the cod in the air fryer. Do not stack. Cook in batches. Spray with cooking oil. Cook for 8 minutes.
5. Open the air fryer and flip the cod. Cook for an additional 7 minutes.
6. Remove the cooked cod from the air fryer, then repeat steps 4 and 5 for the remaining fillets.
7. Serve with Classic French Fries or prepare air-fried frozen fries. Frozen fries will need to be cooked for 18 to 20 minutes at 400ºF.
8. Cool before serving.

Pasta Shrimp

Servings: 4
Cooking Time: 5 Minutes
Ingredients:
- ½ teaspoon hot paprika
- 2 garlic cloves, peeled and minced
- 1 teaspoon onion powder
- ½ teaspoon salt
- 1 teaspoon lemon-pepper seasoning
- 18 shrimps, shelled and deveined
- 2 tablespoons extra-virgin olive oil
- ¼ teaspoon cumin powder
- 2 tablespoons squeezed lemon juice
- ½ cup parsley, coarsely chopped

Directions:
1. Thoroughly mix the ingredients in a medium-size bowl, then cover it with a foil and refrigerate for 30-45 minutes.
2. Place the shrimps in the basket that has been coated with cooking oil or spray.
3. Arrange the basket to the air fryer and cook at 400 degrees F/ 205 degrees C for 5 minutes or until turn pink.
4. Serve warm with cooked pasta or just shrimps!

Creamy Tuna With Zucchinis

Servings: 4
Cooking Time: 20 Minutes
Ingredients:
- 4 medium zucchinis
- 120g of tuna in oil canned drained
- 30g grated cheese
- 1 teaspoon pine nuts
- Salt, black pepper to taste

Directions:
1. Cut the zucchini in ½ laterally and empty it with a small spoon set aside the pulp that will be used for filling; place them in the basket.
2. In a food processor, put the zucchini pulp, drained tuna, pine nuts and grated cheese.
3. Mix until you get a homogeneous and dense mixture.
4. Fill the zucchini. Set the air fryer to 360 degrees F/ 180 degrees C.
5. Air fry for almost 20 minutes depending on the size of the zucchini. Let cool before serving.

Cajun Fish Cakes

Servings: 4
Cooking Time: 30 Minutes
Ingredients:
- 2 catfish fillets
- 1 cup all-purpose flour
- 1 ounce butter
- 1 teaspoon baking powder
- 1 teaspoon baking soda
- ½ cup buttermilk
- 1 teaspoon Cajun seasoning
- 1 cup Swiss cheese, shredded

Directions:
1. Boil a pot of water, the put in the fish fillets and boil for 5 minutes or until it is opaque.
2. When done, flake the fish into small pieces.
3. In a bowl, mix up the other ingredients, then add the fish and mix them well.
4. Form 12 fish patties from the mixture.
5. Place the patties to the cooking pan and arrange the pan to your air fryer.
6. Cook at 380 degrees F/ 195 degrees C for 15 minutes.
7. Working in batches is suggested.
8. Enjoy!

Ginger Salmon Fillet

Servings: 4
Cooking Time: 22 Minutes
Ingredients:
- 2 salmon fillets
- 60g cane sugar
- 4 tablespoons soy sauce
- 50g sesame seeds
- Unlimited Ginger

Directions:
1. Preheat the air fryer at about 360 degrees F/ 180 degrees C for 5 minutes.
2. Put the sugar and soy sauce in the basket.
3. Cook everything for 5 minutes.
4. In the meantime, wash the fish well, pass it through sesame to cover it completely and place it inside the tank and add the fresh ginger.
5. Cook for 12 minutes.
6. Flip the salmon fillets and finish cooking for another 8 minutes.

Snapper Scampi

Servings: 4
Cooking Time: 8 To 10 Minutes
Ingredients:
- 4 (6-ounce) skinless snapper or arctic char fillets
- 1 tablespoon olive oil
- 3 tablespoons lemon juice, divided
- ½ teaspoon dried basil
- Pinch salt
- Freshly ground black pepper
- 2 tablespoons butter
- 2 cloves garlic, minced

Directions:
1. Rub the fish fillets with olive oil and 1 tablespoon of the lemon juice. Sprinkle with the basil, salt, and pepper, and place in the air fryer basket.
2. Grill the fish for 7 to 8 minutes or until the fish just flakes when tested with a fork. Remove the fish from the basket and put on a serving plate. Cover to keep warm.
3. In a 6-by-6-by-2-inch pan, combine the butter, remaining 2 tablespoons lemon juice, and garlic. Cook in the air fryer for 1 to 2 minutes or until the garlic is sizzling. Pour this mixture over the fish and serve.
4. Did You Know? You can buy bottled lemon and lime juice at the supermarket, but for recipes such as this one, where the flavor is so important, squeeze the juice from a lemon yourself just before you make the recipe.

Typical Cod Nuggets

Servings: 4
Cooking Time: 10 Minutes
Ingredients:
- 16-ounce cod
- To make the breading:
- 1 cup all-purpose flour
- 2 tablespoons olive oil
- 2 eggs, beaten
- 1 pinch salt
- ¾ cup panko breadcrumbs, finely processed

Directions:
1. Thoroughly mix the oil, salt and crumbs in a medium-size bowl.
2. Take the cod, make pieces from it of about 5 inches by 1 inch.
3. In a bowl of medium size, thoroughly mix the salt, oil and crumbs.
4. Side by side place three bowls; add the flour in the first bowl, crumb mixture in the second and eggs in the third. Dip the fish in the flour, one by one, and then mix in the egg mix.
5. Lastly coat with the crumb mixture completely.
6. Place the fish pieces in the basket that has been coated with cooking oil or spray.
7. Arrange the basket to the air fryer and cook at 390 degrees F/ 200 degrees C for 10 minutes or until turn pink.
8. Serve the crispy fish!

Blackened Shrimp

Servings: 4
Cooking Time: 10 Minutes

Ingredients:
- 1 pound raw shrimp, peeled and deveined (see Prep tip, here)
- 1 teaspoon paprika
- ½ teaspoon dried oregano
- ½ teaspoon cayenne pepper
- Juice of ½ lemon
- Salt
- Pepper
- Cooking oil

Directions:
1. Place the shrimp in a sealable plastic bag and add the paprika, oregano, cayenne pepper, lemon juice, and salt and pepper to taste. Seal the bag and shake well to combine.
2. Spray a grill pan or the air fryer basket with cooking oil.
3. Place the shrimp in the air fryer. It is okay to stack the shrimp. Cook for 4 minutes.
4. Open the air fryer and shake the basket. Cook for an additional 3 to 4 minutes, or until the shrimp has blackened.
5. Cool before serving.

Flounder Filets With Parmesan Cheese

Servings: 3
Cooking Time: 10 Minutes

Ingredients:
- 1 pound flounder filets
- 1 teaspoon garlic, minced
- 2 tablespoons soy sauce
- 1 teaspoon Dijon mustard
- ¼ cup malt vinegar
- 1 teaspoon granulated sugar
- Salt and black pepper, to taste
- ½ cup plain flour
- 1 egg
- 2 tablespoons milk
- ½ cup parmesan cheese, grated

Directions:
1. In a suitable bowl, combine the flounder filets with garlic, soy sauce, mustard, vinegar and sugar.
2. Marinate the flounder filets by refrigerating it for at least 1 hour.
3. When marinated, take the flounder filets out of the marinade and season with salt and pepper.
4. Place the plain flour in a suitable shallow bowl.
5. In another bowl, beat the egg and add milk until pale and well combined, then in the third bowl, place the Parmesan cheese.
6. Coat the flounder filet with the flour, egg mixture and Parmesan in order, pressing to adhere.
7. Coat the remaining flounder filets with the same steps.
8. Cook the flounder filets in the preheated Air Fryer at 400 degrees F/ 205 degrees C for 10 minutes, flipping halfway through.
9. When done, serve and enjoy.

Flavor Moroccan Harissa Shrimp

Servings: 3
Cooking Time: 10 Minutes
Ingredients:
- 1-pound breaded shrimp, frozen
- 1 teaspoon extra-virgin olive oil
- Sea salt, to taste
- Ground black pepper, to taste
- 1 teaspoon coriander seeds
- 1 teaspoon caraway seeds
- 1 teaspoon crushed red pepper
- 1 teaspoon fresh garlic, minced

Directions:
1. Arrange the breaded shrimp tossed with olive oil to the cooking basket and then arrange the basket to the air fryer.
2. Cook the shrimp at 400 degrees F/ 205 degrees C for 5 minutes.
3. After 5 minutes, shake the basket and cook an additional 4 minutes.
4. During cooking, mix the remaining ingredients until well combined.
5. Taste and adjust seasonings.
6. Toss the warm shrimp with the harissa sauce and serve immediately. Enjoy!

Parmesan Cod With Onion

Servings: 4
Cooking Time: 14 Minutes
Ingredients:
- 4 cod fillets, boneless
- Black pepper and salt to the taste
- 1 cup parmesan
- 4 tablespoons balsamic vinegar
- A drizzle of olive oil
- 3 spring onions, chopped

Directions:
1. Season fish with salt, black pepper, grease with the oil, and coat it in parmesan.
2. Put the fillets in your air fryer basket and cook at almost 370 degrees F/ 185 degrees C for 14 minutes.
3. Meanwhile, in a suitable bowl, mix the spring onions with salt, black pepper and the vinegar and whisk.
4. Divide the cod between plates, drizzle the spring onions mix all over and serve with a side salad.

Old Bay Cod Fish Fillets

Servings: 2
Cooking Time: 12 Minutes
Ingredients:
- 2 cod fish fillets
- 1 teaspoon butter, melted
- 1 teaspoon Old Bay seasoning
- 1 egg, beaten
- 2 tablespoons coconut milk, unsweetened
- ⅓ cup coconut flour, unsweetened

Directions:
1. Prepare a Ziploc bag, add the cod fish fillets, butter and Old Bay seasoning, shake to coat the fillets well on all sides.
2. Whisk the egg and coconut milk until frothy in a shallow bowl.
3. In another bowl, place the coconut flour.
4. Coat the fish fillets with the egg mixture and coconut flour in order, pressing to adhere.
5. Cook the fish fillets at 390 degrees F/ 200 degrees C until the fish fillets flake easily when poking it with a fork, for 12 minutes.
6. Flip halfway through.
7. Bon appétit!

Simple Fish Sticks

Servings: 2
Cooking Time: 10 Minutes
Ingredients:
- ½ pound fish sticks, frozen
- ½ pound Vidalia onions, halved
- 1 teaspoon sesame oil
- Sea salt, to taste
- Ground black pepper, to taste
- ½ teaspoon red pepper flakes
- 4 tablespoons mayonnaise
- 4 tablespoons Greek-style yogurt
- ¼ teaspoon mustard seeds
- 1 teaspoon chipotle chili in adobo, minced

Directions:
1. Drizzle the fish sticks and Vidalia onions with sesame oil.
2. Toss the fish sticks with red pepper flakes, salt and black pepper.
3. Transfer the fish sticks to the cooking basket and arrange the basket to the air fryer.
4. Cook the fish sticks and onions at 400 degrees F/ 205 degrees C for 10 minutes, shaking the basket halfway through.
5. Mix up the mayonnaise, Greek-style yogurt, mustard seeds and chipotle chili at the same time.
6. Garnish the warm sticks with Vidalia onions and the sauce on the side.
7. Bon appétit!

Grouper With Miso-honey Sauce

Servings: 2
Cooking Time: 10 Minutes
Ingredients:
- ¾ pound grouper fillets
- Salt and white pepper, to taste
- 1 tablespoon sesame oil
- 1 teaspoon water
- 1 teaspoon deli mustard or Dijon mustard
- ¼ cup white miso
- 1 tablespoon mirin
- 1 tablespoon honey
- 1 tablespoon Shoyu sauce

Directions:
1. Sprinkle salt and white pepper on the grouper fillets, then drizzle them with a nonstick cooking oil.
2. Arrange the fillets to the air fryer and cook them at 400 degrees F/ 205 degrees C for 10 minutes, flipping halfway through.
3. Meanwhile, whisk the other ingredients to make the sauce.
4. Serve the warm fish with the miso-honey sauce on the side. Bon appétit!

Spiced Shrimp With Zucchini

Servings: 4
Cooking Time: 25 Minutes
Ingredients:
- 2 zucchinis
- 30 shrimp
- 7 cherry tomatoes
- Black pepper and salt to taste
- 1 garlic clove

Directions:
1. Pour the oil in the air fryer, add the garlic clove and diced zucchini.
2. Cook for almost 15 minutes at 300 degrees F/ 150 degrees C.
3. Add the shrimp and the pieces of tomato, salt, and spices.
4. Cook for another 5 to 10 minutes or until the shrimp water evaporates.

Tuna And Fruit Kebabs

Servings: 4
Cooking Time:8 To 12 Minutes
Ingredients:
- 1 pound tuna steaks, cut into 1-inch cubes
- ½ cup canned pineapple chunks, drained, juice reserved
- ½ cup large red grapes
- 1 tablespoon honey
- 2 teaspoons grated fresh ginger
- 1 teaspoon olive oil
- Pinch cayenne pepper

Directions:
1. Thread the tuna, pineapple, and grapes on 8 bamboo (see Tip) or 4 metal skewers that fit in the air fryer.
2. In a small bowl, whisk the honey, 1 tablespoon of reserved pineapple juice, the ginger, olive oil, and cayenne. Brush this mixture over the kebabs. Let them stand for 10 minutes.
3. Grill the kebabs for 8 to 12 minutes, or until the tuna reaches an internal temperature of at least 145°F on a meat thermometer, and the fruit is tender and glazed, brushing once with the remaining sauce. Discard any remaining marinade. Serve immediately.

Ginger Mushroom Flounder

Servings: 4
Cooking Time: 15 Minutes
Ingredients:
- 4 flounder fillets, boneless
- 2 tablespoons coconut aminos
- A pinch of black pepper and salt
- 1 and ½ teaspoons. ginger, grated
- 2 teaspoons olive oil
- 2 green onions, chopped
- 2 cups mushrooms, sliced

Directions:
1. Heat a suitable pan that fits your air fryer with the oil over medium-high heat, add the mushrooms and all the other ingredients except the fish, toss and sauté for 5 minutes.
2. Add the fish, toss gently, introduce the pan in the air fryer and cook at almost 390 degrees F/ 200 degrees C for almost 10 minutes.
3. Serve.

Scallops With Green Vegetables

Servings: 4
Cooking Time:8 To 11 Minutes
Ingredients:
- 1 cup green beans
- 1 cup frozen peas
- 1 cup frozen chopped broccoli
- 2 teaspoons olive oil
- ½ teaspoon dried basil
- ½ teaspoon dried oregano
- 12 ounces sea scallops (see Tip)

Directions:
1. In a large bowl, toss the green beans, peas, and broccoli with the olive oil. Place in the air fryer basket. Air-fry for 4 to 6 minutes, or until the vegetables are crisp-tender.
2. Remove the vegetables from the air fryer basket and sprinkle with the herbs. Set aside.
3. In the air fryer basket, put the scallops and air-fry for 4 to 5 minutes, or until the scallops are firm and reach an internal temperature of just 145°F on a meat thermometer.
4. Toss scallops with the vegetables and serve immediately.

Vegetable Side Dishes Recipes
Sriracha Golden Cauliflower

Servings:4
Cooking Time: 17 Minutes
Ingredients:
- ¼ cup vegan butter, melted
- ¼ cup sriracha sauce
- 4 cups cauliflower florets
- 1 cup bread crumbs
- 1 teaspoon salt

Directions:
1. Preheat the air fryer to 375ºF (191ºC).
2. Mix the sriracha and vegan butter in a bowl and pour this mixture over the cauliflower, taking care to cover each floret entirely.
3. In a separate bowl, combine the bread crumbs and salt.
4. Dip the cauliflower florets in the bread crumbs, coating each one well. Air fry in the air fryer for 17 minutes.
5. Serve hot.

Basmati Risotto

Servings: 2
Cooking Time: 30 Minutes
Ingredients:
- 1 onion, diced
- 1 small carrot, diced
- 2 cups vegetable broth, boiling
- ½ cup grated Cheddar cheese
- 1 clove garlic, minced
- ¾ cup long-grain basmati rice
- 1 tablespoon olive oil
- 1 tablespoon unsalted butter

Directions:
1. Preheat the air fryer to 390°F (199°C).
2. Grease a baking tin with oil and stir in the butter, garlic, carrot, and onion.
3. Put the tin in the air fryer and bake for 4 minutes.
4. Pour in the rice and bake for a further 4 minutes, stirring three times throughout the baking time.
5. Turn the temperature down to 320°F (160°C).
6. Add the vegetable broth and give the dish a gentle stir. Bake for 22 minutes, leaving the air fryer uncovered.
7. Pour in the cheese, stir once more and serve.

Creamy Cauliflower Puree

Servings: 2
Cooking Time: 8 Minutes
Ingredients:
- 1 ½ cup cauliflower, chopped
- 1 tablespoon butter, melted
- ½ teaspoon salt
- 1 tablespoon fresh parsley, chopped
- ¼ cup heavy cream
- Cooking spray

Directions:
1. Spritz the cooking spray over the inside of the air fryer basket.
2. Place the chopped cauliflower in the air fryer basket.
3. Cook in your air fryer at 400 degrees F/ 205 degrees C for 8 minutes. Stir the cauliflower every 4 minutes.
4. Heat the heavy cream until it is hot. Then pour in a blender, add parsley, butter, salt, and cauliflower.
5. Blend until it is smooth.

Lemon Cabbage With Cilantro

Servings: 4
Cooking Time: 25 Minutes
Ingredients:
- 1 green cabbage head, shredded and cut into large wedges
- 2 tablespoons olive oil
- 1 tablespoon cilantro, chopped
- 1 tablespoon lemon juice
- A pinch of salt and black pepper

Directions:
1. Before cooking, heat your air fryer to 370 degrees F/ 185 degrees C.
2. In the air fryer basket, mix all the ingredients.
3. Cook in your air fryer for 25 minutes.
4. Serve on plates as a side dish.

Flavorful Radish Salad

Servings: 4
Cooking Time: 30 Minutes
Ingredients:
- 1 ½ pounds radishes, trimmed and halved
- 2 tablespoons olive oil
- Pepper and salt, as needed
- For the Salad:
- 1 teaspoon olive oil
- 1 tablespoon balsamic vinegar
- ½ pound mozzarella, sliced
- 1 teaspoon honey
- Pepper and salt, as needed

Directions:
1. Mix thoroughly the salt, black pepper, oil, and the radishes in medium sized bowl.
2. On a flat kitchen surface, plug your air fryer and turn it on.
3. Before cooking, heat your air fryer to 350 degrees F/ 175 degrees C for 4 to 5 minutes.
4. Place the mixture onto the air fryer basket.
5. Cook in your air fryer for 3 minutes.
6. In another medium sized bowl, mix thoroughly the cheese and fried radish.
7. Mix the remaining ingredients in a small bowl. Drizzle over the salad to serve.

Parsley Cabbage

Servings: 4
Cooking Time: 20 Minutes
Ingredients:
- 2 ounces butter, melted
- 1 green cabbage head, shredded 1 and ½ cups heavy cream
- ¼ cup parsley, chopped
- 1 tablespoon sweet paprika
- 1 teaspoon lemon zest, grated

Directions:
1. Heat butter on a suitable cooking pan.
2. Then add cabbage and cook for 5 minutes.
3. Place the remaining ingredients in the pan. Toss well and transfer the pan into your air fryer.
4. Cook in your air fryer at 380 degrees F/ 195 degrees C for 5 minutes.
5. Serve on plates as a side dish.

Curried Brussels Sprouts

Servings: 4
Cooking Time:15 To 17 Minutes
Ingredients:
- 1 pound Brussels sprouts, ends trimmed, discolored leaves removed, halved lengthwise
- 2 teaspoons olive oil
- 3 teaspoons curry powder, divided
- 1 tablespoon freshly squeezed lemon juice

Directions:
1. In a large bowl, toss the Brussels sprouts with the olive oil and 1 teaspoon of curry powder. Transfer to the air fryer basket. Roast for 12 minutes, shaking the basket once during cooking.
2. Sprinkle with the remaining 2 teaspoons of the curry powder and the lemon juice. Shake again. Roast for 3 to 5 minutes more, or until the Brussels sprouts are browned and crisp (see Tip). Serve immediately.

Spinach And Cheese–stuffed Mushrooms

Servings: 4
Cooking Time: 10 Minutes

Ingredients:

- Olive oil
- 4 ounces reduced-fat cream cheese, softened
- ¾ cup shredded Italian blend cheese
- ¼ cup whole-wheat bread crumbs
- 1 egg
- ¼ teaspoon salt
- ¼ teaspoon freshly ground black pepper
- 1 cup fresh baby spinach, chopped
- 20 large mushrooms, stems removed

Directions:

1. Spray a fryer basket lightly with olive oil.
2. In a medium bowl, use an electric mixer to combine the cream cheese, Italian blend cheese, bread crumbs, egg, salt, and pepper.
3. Add the spinach and stir with a spoon to combine.
4. Spoon the mixture into each mushroom, pressing the mixture into the mushroom and leaving a little bit popping out of the top.
5. Place the stuffed mushrooms in a single layer in the fryer basket. Spray lightly with olive oil. You may need to cook these in more than one batch.
6. Air fry until the mushrooms have started to brown lightly and the cheese is lightly brown on top, 7 to 10 minutes.

Cheddar Mushroom Cakes

Servings: 4
Cooking Time: 8 Minutes

Ingredients:

- 9 ounces mushrooms, finely chopped
- ¼ cup coconut flour
- 1 teaspoon salt
- 1 egg, beaten
- 3 ounces Cheddar cheese, shredded
- 1 teaspoon dried parsley
- ½ teaspoon ground black pepper
- 1 teaspoon sesame oil
- 1 ounce spring onion, chopped

Directions:

1. Mix the coconut flour, salt, dried parsley, minced onion, ground black pepper, egg, and the chopped mushrooms until smooth.
2. Then add Cheddar cheese. Use a fork to stir.
3. Before cooking, heat your air fryer to 385 degrees F/ 195 degrees C.
4. Line baking paper over the air fryer pan.
5. Use a spoon to make medium-size patties from the mixture. Then arrange evenly on the pan.
6. Sprinkle the patties with sesame oil and cook in your air fryer for 4 minutes from each side.

Maple Glazed Parsnips

Servings: 6
Cooking Time: 44 Minutes
Ingredients:

- 2 pounds parsnips, peeled
- 1 tablespoon butter, melted
- 2 tablespoons maple syrup
- 1 tablespoon dried parsley flakes, crushed
- ¼ teaspoon red pepper flakes, crushed

Directions:
1. Before cooking, heat your air fryer to 355 degrees F/ 180 degrees C.
2. Using cooking spray, spray the air fryer basket. Cut the peeled parsnips into 1-inch chunks.
3. In a bowl, add butter and parsnips and toss well to coat.
4. Then evenly arrange the parsnips on the air fryer basket.
5. Cook in your air fryer for about 40 minutes.
6. Then mix the remaining ingredients in a large bowl.
7. Transfer the mixture inside the air fryer basket.
8. Cook for about 4 minutes or more.
9. When cooked, remove from the air fryer and serve warm.

Gorgonzola Mushrooms With Horseradish Mayo

Servings:5
Cooking Time: 10 Minutes
Ingredients:

- ½ cup bread crumbs
- 2 cloves garlic, pressed
- 2 tablespoons chopped fresh coriander
- ⅓ teaspoon kosher salt
- ½ teaspoon crushed red pepper flakes
- 1½ tablespoons olive oil
- 20 medium mushrooms, stems removed
- ½ cup grated Gorgonzola cheese
- ¼ cup low-fat mayonnaise
- 1 teaspoon prepared horseradish, well-drained
- 1 tablespoon finely chopped fresh parsley

Directions:
1. Preheat the air fryer to 380ºF (193ºC).
2. Combine the bread crumbs together with the garlic, coriander, salt, red pepper, and olive oil.
3. Take equal-sized amounts of the breadcrumb mixture and use them to stuff the mushroom caps. Add the grated Gorgonzola on top of each.
4. Put the mushrooms in the air fryer baking pan and transfer to the air fryer.
5. Air fry for 10 minutes, ensuring the stuffing is warm throughout.
6. In the meantime, prepare the horseradish mayo. Mix the mayonnaise, horseradish and parsley.
7. When the mushrooms are ready, serve with the mayo.

Apple Brussel Sprout Salad

Servings: 4
Cooking Time: 15 Minutes
Ingredients:

- 1 pound Brussels sprouts
- 1 apple, cored and diced
- ½ cup mozzarella cheese, crumbled
- ½ cup pomegranate seeds
- 1 small-sized red onion, chopped
- 4 eggs, hardboiled and sliced
- Dressing:
- ¼ cup olive oil
- 2 tablespoons champagne vinegar
- 1 teaspoon Dijon mustard
- 1 teaspoon honey
- Salt and black pepper, to taste

Directions:
1. At 380 degrees F/ 195 degrees C, preheat your air fryer.
2. Add the Brussels sprouts to the cooking basket.
3. Spritz with cooking spray and cook for almost 15 minutes.
4. Toss the Brussels sprouts with the apple, cheese, pomegranate seeds, and red onion.
5. Mix all the recipe ingredients for the dressing and toss to combine well.
6. Serve topped with the hard-boiled eggs. Serve

Sweet And Spicy Tofu

Servings: 3
Cooking Time: 23 Minutes
Ingredients:

- For Tofu:
- 1 (14-ounce) block firm tofu, pressed and cubed
- ½ cup arrowroot flour
- ½ teaspoon sesame oil
- For Sauce:
- 4 tablespoons low-sodium soy sauce
- 1½ tablespoons rice vinegar
- 1½ tablespoons chili sauce
- 1 tablespoon agave nectar
- 2 large garlic cloves, minced
- 1 teaspoon fresh ginger, peeled and grated
- 2 scallions (green part), chopped

Directions:
1. Mix arrowroot flour, sesame oil, and tofu together in a bowl.
2. Before cooking, heat your air fryer to 360 degrees F/ 180 degrees C.
3. Gently grease an air fryer basket.
4. Place the tofu evenly on the air fryer basket in a layer.
5. Cook in your air fryer for 20 minutes. Halfway through cooking, shake the air fryer basket once.
6. To make the sauce, add soy sauce, rice vinegar, chili sauce, agave nectar, garlic, and ginger in a bowl. Beat the mixture to combine well.
7. When the tofu has cooked, remove from the air fryer and transfer to a skillet.
8. Add the sauce and heat the skillet over medium heat. Cook for about 3 minutes. Stir the meal from time to time.
9. Add the scallions to garnish and serve hot.

Spicy Cauliflower Roast

Servings: 4
Cooking Time: 20 Minutes
Ingredients:
- Cauliflower:
- 5 cups cauliflower florets
- 3 tablespoons vegetable oil
- ½ teaspoon ground cumin
- ½ teaspoon ground coriander
- ½ teaspoon kosher salt
- Sauce:
- ½ cup Greek yogurt or sour cream
- ¼ cup chopped fresh cilantro
- 1 jalapeño, coarsely chopped
- 4 cloves garlic, peeled
- ½ teaspoon kosher salt
- 2 tablespoons water

Directions:
1. Preheat the air fryer to 400ºF (204ºC).
2. In a large bowl, combine the cauliflower, oil, cumin, coriander, and salt. Toss to coat.
3. Put the cauliflower in the air fryer basket. Roast for 20 minutes, stirring halfway through the roasting time.
4. Meanwhile, in a blender, combine the yogurt, cilantro, jalapeño, garlic, and salt. Blend, adding the water as needed to keep the blades moving and to thin the sauce.
5. At the end of roasting time, transfer the cauliflower to a large serving bowl. Pour the sauce over and toss gently to coat. Serve immediately.

Zucchini Tots With Mozzarella

Servings: 4
Cooking Time: 6 Minutes
Ingredients:
- 1 zucchini, grated
- ½ cup Mozzarella, shredded
- 1 egg, beaten
- 2 tablespoons. almond flour
- ½ teaspoon black pepper
- 1 teaspoon coconut oil, melted

Directions:
1. Mix up grated zucchini, shredded Mozzarella, egg, almond flour, and black pepper.
2. Then make the small zucchini tots with the help of the fingertips.
3. At 385 degrees F/ 195 degrees C, preheat your air fryer.
4. Place the zucchini tots in the air fryer basket and cook for 3 minutes from each side or until the zucchini tots are golden brown.
5. Serve.

Balsamic Sautéed Greens

Servings: 4
Cooking Time: 15 Minutes
Ingredients:
- 1 pound collard greens
- ¼ cup cherry tomatoes, halved
- 1 tablespoon balsamic vinegar
- A pinch of black pepper and salt
- 2 tablespoons chicken stock

Directions:
1. In a suitable pan that fits your air fryer, mix the collard greens with the other ingredients, toss gently, introduce in the preheated air fryer, and cook at almost 360 degrees F/ 180 degrees C for almost 15 minutes.
2. Serve.

Super Veg Rolls

Servings: 6
Cooking Time: 10 Minutes
Ingredients:
- 2 potatoes, mashed
- ¼ cup peas
- ¼ cup mashed carrots
- 1 small cabbage, sliced
- ¼ cups beans
- 2 tablespoons sweetcorn
- 1 small onion, chopped
- ½ cup bread crumbs
- 1 packet spring roll sheets
- ½ cup cornstarch slurry

Directions:
1. Preheat the air fryer to 390ºF (199ºC).
2. Boil all the vegetables in water over a low heat. Rinse and allow to dry.
3. Unroll the spring roll sheets and spoon equal amounts of vegetable onto the center of each one. Fold into spring rolls and coat each one with the slurry and bread crumbs.
4. Air fry the rolls in the preheated air fryer for 10 minutes.
5. Serve warm.

Marinara Pepperoni Mushroom Pizza

Servings:4
Cooking Time: 18 Minutes

Ingredients:

- 4 large portobello mushrooms, stems removed
- 4 teaspoons olive oil
- 1 cup marinara sauce
- 1 cup shredded Mozzarella cheese
- 10 slices sugar-free pepperoni

Directions:

1. Preheat the air fryer to 375°F (191°C).
2. Brush each mushroom cap with the olive oil, one teaspoon for each cap.
3. Put on a baking sheet and bake, stem-side down, for 8 minutes.
4. Take out of the air fryer and divide the marinara sauce, Mozzarella cheese and pepperoni evenly among the caps.
5. Air fry for another 10 minutes until browned.
6. Serve hot.

Golden Pickles

Servings:4
Cooking Time: 15 Minutes

Ingredients:

- 14 dill pickles, sliced
- ¼ cup flour
- ⅛ teaspoon baking powder
- Pinch of salt
- 2 tablespoons cornstarch plus 3 tablespoons water
- 6 tablespoons panko bread crumbs
- ½ teaspoon paprika
- Cooking spray

Directions:

1. Preheat the air fryer to 400°F (204°C).
2. Drain any excess moisture out of the dill pickles on a paper towel.
3. In a bowl, combine the flour, baking powder and salt.
4. Throw in the cornstarch and water mixture and combine well with a whisk.
5. Put the panko bread crumbs in a shallow dish along with the paprika. Mix thoroughly.
6. Dip the pickles in the flour batter, before coating in the bread crumbs. Spritz all the pickles with the cooking spray.
7. Transfer to the air fryer basket and air fry for 15 minutes, or until golden brown.
8. Serve immediately.

Asparagus With Garlic

Servings: 4
Cooking Time:4 To 5 Minutes, Or 8 To 11 Minutes Depending On Desired Texture

Ingredients:
- 1 pound asparagus, rinsed, ends snapped off where they naturally break (see Tip)
- 2 teaspoons olive oil
- 3 garlic cloves, minced
- 2 tablespoons balsamic vinegar
- ½ teaspoon dried thyme

Directions:
1. In a large bowl, toss the asparagus with the olive oil. Transfer to the air fryer basket.
2. Sprinkle with garlic. Roast for 4 to 5 minutes for crisp-tender or for 8 to 11 minutes for asparagus that is crisp on the outside and tender on the inside.
3. Drizzle with the balsamic vinegar and sprinkle with the thyme leaves. Serve immediately.

Herb-roasted Vegetables

Servings: 4
Cooking Time:14 To 18 Minutes

Ingredients:
- 1 red bell pepper, sliced
- 1 (8-ounce) package sliced mushrooms
- 1 cup green beans, cut into 2-inch pieces
- ⅓ cup diced red onion
- 3 garlic cloves, sliced
- 1 teaspoon olive oil (see Tip)
- ½ teaspoon dried basil
- ½ teaspoon dried tarragon

Directions:
1. In a medium bowl, mix the red bell pepper, mushrooms, green beans, red onion, and garlic. Drizzle with the olive oil. Toss to coat.
2. Add the herbs and toss again.
3. Place the vegetables in the air fryer basket. Roast for 14 to 18 minutes, or until tender. Serve immediately.

Turmeric Cauliflower Patties

Servings: 2
Cooking Time: 10 Minutes
Ingredients:

- ¼ cup cauliflower, shredded
- 1 egg yolk
- ½ teaspoon ground turmeric
- ¼ teaspoon onion powder
- ¼ teaspoon salt
- 2 ounces Cheddar cheese, shredded
- ¼ teaspoon baking powder
- 1 teaspoon heavy cream
- 1 tablespoon coconut flakes
- Cooking spray

Directions:
1. Squeeze the shredded cauliflower and put it in the bowl.
2. Add egg yolk, ground turmeric, baking powder, onion powder, heavy cream, salt, and coconut flakes.
3. Then melt Cheddar cheese and add it in the cauliflower mixture.
4. Stir the ingredients until you get the smooth mass.
5. After this, make the medium size cauliflower patties.
6. At 365 degrees F/ 185 degrees C, preheat your air fryer.
7. Grease its air fryer basket with cooking spray and put the patties inside.
8. Cook them for almost 5 minutes from each side.
9. Serve warm.

Desserts And Sweets
Banana And Walnut Cake

Servings:6
Cooking Time: 25 Minutes
Ingredients:

- 1 pound (454 g) bananas, mashed
- 8 ounces (227 g) flour
- 6 ounces (170 g) sugar
- 3.5 ounces (99 g) walnuts, chopped
- 2.5 ounces (71 g) butter, melted
- 2 eggs, lightly beaten
- ¼ teaspoon baking soda

Directions:
1. Preheat the air fryer to 355ºF (179ºC).
2. In a bowl, combine the sugar, butter, egg, flour, and baking soda with a whisk. Stir in the bananas and walnuts.
3. Transfer the mixture to a greased baking dish. Put the dish in the air fryer and bake for 10 minutes.
4. Reduce the temperature to 330ºF (166ºC) and bake for another 15 minutes. Serve hot.

Vanilla Berry Cobbler

Servings: 6
Cooking Time: 10 Minutes
Ingredients:
- 1 egg, lightly beaten
- 1 tablespoon butter, melted
- 2 teaspoons swerve
- ½ teaspoon vanilla
- 1 cup almond flour
- ½ cup raspberries, sliced
- ½ cup strawberries, sliced

Directions:
1. Before cooking, heat your air fryer to 360 degrees F/ 180 degrees C.
2. Combine the sliced raspberries and strawberries in an air fryer baking dish that fits in your air fryer.
3. Pour the sweetener over the berries.
4. In a separate bowl, combine together vanilla, butter, and almond flour.
5. Combine the almond flour mixture with the beaten egg.
6. Top the sliced berries with the almond flour mixture and then use foil to cover the dish.
7. Then transfer the dish inside your air fryer and cook at 360 degrees F/ 180 degrees C for 10 minutes.
8. When cooked, remove from the air fryer and serve.

Chocolate Peanut Butter Molten Cupcakes

Servings:8
Cooking Time: 10 To 13 Minutes
Ingredients:
- Nonstick baking spray with flour
- 1⅓ cups chocolate cake mix (from 15-ounce box)
- 1 egg
- 1 egg yolk
- ¼ cup safflower oil
- ¼ cup hot water
- ⅓ cup sour cream
- 3 tablespoons peanut butter
- 1 tablespoon powdered sugar

Directions:
1. Double up 16 foil muffin cups to make 8 cups. Spray each lightly with nonstick spray; set aside.
2. In a medium bowl, combine the cake mix, egg, egg yolk, safflower oil, water, and sour cream, and beat until combined.
3. In a small bowl, combine the peanut butter and powdered sugar and mix well. Form this mixture into 8 balls.
4. Spoon about ¼ cup of the chocolate batter into each muffin cup and top with a peanut butter ball. Spoon remaining batter on top of the peanut butter balls to cover them.
5. Arrange the cups in the air fryer basket, leaving some space between each. Bake for 10 to 13 minutes or until the tops look dry and set.
6. Let the cupcakes cool for about 10 minutes, then serve warm.

S'mores

Servings: 4 S'mores
Cooking Time: 15 Minutes
Ingredients:
- 4 marshmallows
- 4 graham crackers, divided in half
- 1 milk chocolate, divided

Directions:
1. Put 4 halves of graham crackers into the air fryer basket.
2. Cut off a small piece from the bottom of each marshmallow and put the marshmallow on the crackers, which will help to stick them well.
3. Cook at 375ºF for 7–8 minutes until golden-brown.
4. Add on the top the pieces of chocolate and cover with another half of crackers.
5. Continue cooking for about 2 minutes until the chocolate starts melting.
6. Serve and enjoy your S'mores!

Air Fryer Reduced-sugar Cookies

Servings: 10
Cooking Time: 15 Minutes
Ingredients:
- 1 teaspoon of baking powder
- 1 cup of almond flour
- 3 tablespoons of natural low-calorie sweetener
- 1 large egg
- 3-½ tablespoons raspberry reduced-sugar pre-serves
- 4 tablespoons of softened cream cheese

Directions:
1. In a suitable bowl, add egg, baking powder, flour, sweetener, and cream cheese, mix well until a dough wet forms.
2. Then let the dough chill in the fridge for almost 20 minutes, until dough is cool enough.
3. And then form into balls.
4. Let the air fryer preheat to 400 degrees F/ 205 degrees C, add the parchment paper to the air fryer basket.
5. Make ten balls from the dough and put them in the prepared air fryer basket.
6. With your clean hands, make an indentation from your thumb in the center of every cookie. Add 1 teaspoon of the raspberry preserve in the thumb hole.
7. Air fry in the preheated Air Fryer for 7 minutes, or until light golden brown to your liking.
8. Let the cookies cool completely in the parchment paper for almost 15 minutes, or they will fall apart.

Splenda Carrot Cake

Servings: 8
Cooking Time: 40 Minutes

Ingredients:
- 1 ¼ cups all-purpose flour
- 1 teaspoon pumpkin pie spice
- 1 teaspoon baking powder
- ¾ cup Splenda
- 2 cups carrots, grated
- 2 eggs
- ½ teaspoon baking soda
- ¾ cup canola oil

Directions:
1. At 350 degrees F/ 175 degrees C, preheat your Air Fryer. Spray the cake pan with oil spray.
2. Dust flour over that.
3. In a suitable bowl, combine the baking powder, pumpkin pie spice, flour, and baking soda.
4. Mix the eggs, oil, and sugar alternative in another bowl. Now combine the dry to wet ingredients. Add ½ of the dry ingredients first mix and the other ½ of the dry mixture.
5. Add in the grated carrots.
6. Add the prepared cake batter to the greased cake pan.
7. Place the cake pan in the basket of the air fryer.
8. Let it Air fry for ½ an hour, but do not let the top too brown.
9. If the top is browning, add a piece of foil over the top of the cake.
10. Air fry it until a toothpick comes out clean, 35-40 minutes in total.
11. Let the cake cool down before serving.

Yummy Apple Chips

Servings: 6
Cooking Time: 8 Minutes

Ingredients:
- 3 Granny Smith apples, wash, core and thinly slice
- 1 teaspoon ground cinnamon
- 1 pinch of salt

Directions:
1. In the air fryer basket, add cinnamon, salt, and apple slices together and rub well.
2. Cook in your air fryer at 390 degrees F/ 200 degrees C for 8 minutes. Flip the apple slices halfway through cooking.
3. When cooked, remove from the air fryer and serve.

Vanilla Muffins With Pecans

Servings: 12
Cooking Time: 15 Minutes
Ingredients:
- 4 eggs
- 1 teaspoon vanilla
- ¼ cup almond milk
- 2 tablespoons butter, melted
- ½ cup swerve
- 1 teaspoon psyllium husk
- 1 tablespoon baking powder
- ½ cup pecans, chopped
- ½ teaspoon ground cinnamon
- 2 teaspoons allspice
- 1 ½ cups almond flour

Directions:
1. At 370 degrees F/ 185 degrees C, preheat your air fryer.
2. Beat eggs, almond milk, vanilla, sweetener, and butter in a suitable bowl using a hand mixer until smooth.
3. Add remaining recipe ingredients and mix until well combined.
4. Pour batter into the silicone muffin molds and place into the air fryer basket in batches.
5. Cook muffins for almost 15 minutes.
6. Serve and enjoy.

Buttery Shortbread Sticks

Servings: 10
Cooking Time: 22 Minutes
Ingredients:
- ⅓ cup caster sugar
- 1 2/3 cups plain flour
- ¾ cup butter

Directions:
1. In a suitable bowl, mix the sugar and flour.
2. Add the butter and stir until it makes a smooth dough.
3. Cut the dough into ten equal-sized sticks. With a fork, lightly prick the sticks.
4. Place the sticks into the lightly greased baking pan.
5. Set the cook time to 12 minutes.
6. At 355 degrees F/ 180 degrees C, preheat your air fryer.
7. Arrange the pan in preheat air fry basket and insert it in the air fryer.
8. Place the baking pan to cool for about 5-10 minutes.
9. Serve.

Fluffy Strawberry Cake

Servings: 12
Cooking Time: 30 Minutes
Ingredients:

- ¼ cup butter, melted
- 1 cup powdered erythritol
- 1 teaspoon strawberry extract
- 12 egg whites
- 2 teaspoons cream of tartar
- A pinch of salt

Directions:

1. At 400 degrees F/ 205 degrees C, preheat your air fryer.
2. Beat all the egg whites and cream of tartar.
3. Use a hand mixer and whisk until white and fluffy.
4. Add the rest of the recipe ingredients except for the butter and whisk for another minute.
5. Pour into a suitable baking dish.
6. Place this dish in air fryer basket and cook for 30 minutes at 400 degrees F/ 205 degrees C.
7. Drizzle with melted butter once cooled.

Enticing Chocolate Cake

Servings: 6
Cooking Time: 30 Minutes
Ingredients:

- 2 eggs, beaten
- ⅔ cup sour cream
- 1 cup almond flour
- ⅔ cup swerve
- ⅓ cup coconut oil, softened
- ¼ cup cocoa powder
- 2 tablespoons chocolate chips, unsweetened
- 1 ½ teaspoons baking powder
- 1 teaspoon vanilla extract
- ½ teaspoon pure rum extract
- Chocolate Frosting:
- ½ cup butter, softened
- ¼ cup cocoa powder
- 1 cup powdered swerve
- 2 tablespoons milk

Directions:

1. Mix all the recipe ingredients for the chocolate cake with a hand mixer on low speed.
2. Scrape the batter into a cake pan.
3. Air fry at 330 degrees F/ 165 degrees C for 25 to 30 minutes.
4. Then transfer the cake to a wire rack to cool.
5. Meanwhile, whip the butter and cocoa until smooth.
6. Add the powdered swerve. Slowly and gradually, pour in the milk until your frosting reaches desired consistency.
7. Whip until smooth and fluffy; then, frost the cooled cake.
8. Place the frosted cake in your refrigerator for a couple of hours.
9. Serve well chilled.

Chocolate S'mores

Servings:12
Cooking Time: 3 Minutes
Ingredients:
- 12 whole cinnamon graham crackers
- 2 (1.55-ounce / 44-g) chocolate bars, broken into 12 pieces
- 12 marshmallows

Directions:
1. Preheat the air fryer to 350°F (177°C).
2. Halve each graham cracker into 2 squares.
3. Put 6 graham cracker squares in the air fryer. Do not stack. Put a piece of chocolate into each. Bake for 2 minutes.
4. Open the air fryer and add a marshmallow onto each piece of melted chocolate. Bake for 1 additional minute.
5. Remove the cooked s'mores from the air fryer, then repeat steps 2 and 3 for the remaining 6 s'mores.
6. Top with the remaining graham cracker squares and serve.

Cinnamon Pumpkin Cookies

Servings: 8
Cooking Time: 8 Minutes
Ingredients:
- ¼ cup almond flour
- ½ cup pumpkin puree
- 3 tablespoons swerve
- ½ teaspoon baking soda
- 1 tablespoon coconut flakes
- ½ teaspoon cinnamon
- Pinch of salt

Directions:
1. At 360 degrees F/ 180 degrees C, preheat your air fryer.
2. Add all the recipe ingredients into the bowl and mix until well combined.
3. Grease its air fryer basket with cooking spray.
4. Make cookies from bowl mixture and place into the air fryer and cook for 8 minutes.
5. Serve and enjoy.

Eggless & Vegan Cake

Servings: 8
Cooking Time: 10 Minutes

Ingredients:

- 2 tablespoons olive oil
- ¼ cup all-purpose flour
- 2 tablespoons cocoa powder
- ⅛ teaspoon baking soda
- 3 tablespoons sugar
- 1 tablespoon of warm water
- 3 tablespoons milk:
- 2 drops of vanilla extract
- 4 raw almonds for decoration roughly chopped
- a pinch of salt

Directions:

1. Let the air fryer preheat to 390 degrees F/ 200 degrees C for at least 2 minutes.
2. In a suitable bowl, add sugar, milk, water, and oil. Whisk until a smooth batter forms.
3. Now add salt, all-purpose flour, cocoa powder, and baking soda, sift them into wet ingredients, mix to form a paste.
4. Spray the four-inch baking pan with oil and pour the batter into it. Then add in the chopped up almonds on top of it.
5. Put the baking pan in the preheated air fryer. And cook for 10 minutes.
6. Take out from the air fryer.
7. Let it cool completely before slicing.

Banana Chocolate Muffins

Servings: 8
Cooking Time: 30 Minutes

Ingredients:

- Wet Mix
- 3 tablespoons of milk
- 1 teaspoon of Nutella
- 4 Cavendish size, ripe bananas
- ½ cup sugar
- 1 teaspoon of vanilla essence
- 2 large eggs
- Dry Mix
- 1 teaspoon of baking powder
- 1 ¼ cup of whole wheat flour
- 1 teaspoon of baking soda
- 1 teaspoon of cinnamon
- 2 tablespoons of cocoa powder
- 1 teaspoon of salt
- Optional
- 1 handful chopped walnuts
- Fruits, Dried slices
- Chocolate sprinkles

Directions:

1. With the fork, in a suitable bowl, mash up the bananas, add all the wet ingredients to it, and mix well.
2. Sift all the dry ingredients so they combine well. Add into the wet ingredients. Carefully fold both ingredients together. Do not over mix.
3. Then add in the diced walnuts, slices of dried up fruits, and chocolate sprinkles.
4. Let the air fryer preheat to 250 degrees F/ 120 degrees C.
5. Add the batter into muffin cups before that, spray them with oil generously.
6. Air fryer them for at least ½ an hour, or until a toothpick comes out clean.
7. Serve.

Chocolate Peanut Butter Bread Pudding

Servings: 8
Cooking Time: 10 To 12 Minutes

Ingredients:
- Nonstick baking spray with flour
- 1 egg
- 1 egg yolk
- ¾ cup chocolate milk
- 2 tablespoons cocoa powder
- 3 tablespoons brown sugar
- 3 tablespoons peanut butter
- 1 teaspoon vanilla
- 5 slices firm white bread, cubed

Directions:
1. Spray a 6-by-6-by-2-inch baking pan with nonstick spray.
2. In a medium bowl, combine the egg, egg yolk, chocolate milk, cocoa, brown sugar, peanut butter, and vanilla, and mix until combined. Stir in the bread cubes and let soak for 10 minutes.
3. Spoon this mixture into the prepared pan. Bake for 10 to 12 minutes or until the pudding is firm to the touch.

Sweet Orange Muffins

Servings: 5
Cooking Time: 10 Minutes

Ingredients:
- 5 eggs, beaten
- 1 tablespoon poppy seeds
- 1 teaspoon vanilla extract
- ¼ teaspoon ground nutmeg
- ½ teaspoon baking powder
- 1 teaspoon orange juice
- 1 teaspoon orange zest, grated
- 5 tablespoons coconut flour
- 1 tablespoon Monk fruit
- 2 tablespoons coconut flakes
- Cooking spray

Directions:
1. After adding the eggs, poppy seeds, vanilla extract, ground nutmeg, baking powder, orange juice, orange zest, coconut flour, Monk fruit and coconut flakes, mix them well until homogenous and have no clumps.
2. Spray the inside of the muffin molds.
3. Pour the mixture batter in the molds and then arrange them to the air fryer.
4. Cook them at 360 degrees F/ 180 degrees C for 10 minutes.
5. When cooked, serve and enjoy.

Erythritol Vanilla Butter Pie

Servings: 8
Cooking Time: 20 Minutes
Ingredients:
- 1 egg
- 2 tablespoons erythritol
- ½ cup butter, melted
- 1 teaspoon vanilla
- 1 cup almond flour
- 1 teaspoon baking soda
- 1 tablespoon vinegar

Directions:
1. Mix almond flour and baking soda in a suitable bowl.
2. In a separate bowl, whisk the egg with sweetener and vanilla.
3. Pour whisk egg, vinegar, and butter in almond flour and mix until dough is formed.
4. At 340 degrees F/ 170 degrees C, preheat your air fryer.
5. Roll dough using the rolling pin in air fryer basket size.
6. Place rolled dough in air fryer basket and cook for 20 minutes.
7. Slice and serve.

Cinnamon And Pecan Pie

Servings:4
Cooking Time: 25 Minutes
Ingredients:
- 1 pie dough
- ½ teaspoons cinnamon
- ¾ teaspoon vanilla extract
- 2 eggs
- ¾ cup maple syrup
- ⅛ teaspoon nutmeg
- 3 tablespoons melted butter, divided
- 2 tablespoons sugar
- ½ cup chopped pecans

Directions:
1. Preheat the air fryer to 370°F (188°C).
2. In a small bowl, coat the pecans in 1 tablespoon of melted butter.
3. Transfer the pecans to the air fryer and air fry for about 10 minutes.
4. Put the pie dough in a greased pie pan and add the pecans on top.
5. In a bowl, mix the rest of the ingredients. Pour this over the pecans.
6. Put the pan in the air fryer and bake for 25 minutes.
7. Serve immediately.

Rich Chocolate Cookie

Servings: 4
Cooking Time: 9 Minutes
Ingredients:
- Nonstick baking spray with flour
- 3 tablespoons softened butter
- ⅓ cup plus 1 tablespoon brown sugar
- 1 egg yolk
- ½ cup flour
- 2 tablespoons ground white chocolate
- ¼ teaspoon baking soda
- ½ teaspoon vanilla
- ¾ cup chocolate chips

Directions:
1. Preheat the air fryer to 350ºF (177ºC).
2. In a medium bowl, beat the butter and brown sugar together until fluffy. Stir in the egg yolk.
3. Add the flour, white chocolate, baking soda, and vanilla, and mix well. Stir in the chocolate chips.
4. Line a baking pan with parchment paper. Spray the parchment paper with nonstick baking spray with flour.
5. Spread the batter into the prepared pan, leaving a ½-inch border on all sides.
6. Bake for about 9 minutes or until the cookie is light brown and just barely set.
7. Remove the pan from the air fryer and let cool for 10 minutes. Remove the cookie from the pan, remove the parchment paper, and let cool on a wire rack.
8. Serve immediately.

Fluffy Vanilla Butter Cake

Servings: 8
Cooking Time: 35 Minutes
Ingredients:
- 6 egg yolks
- 3 cups almond flour
- 2 teaspoons vanilla
- 1 egg, lightly beaten
- ¼ cup erythritol
- 1 cup butter
- Pinch of salt

Directions:
1. At 350 degrees F/ 175 degrees C, preheat your air fryer.
2. In a suitable bowl, beat butter and sweetener until fluffy.
3. Add the vanilla and 6 egg yolks and beat them together until well combined.
4. Add remaining ingredients and beat until combined.
5. Pour batter into air fryer cake pan and place into the air fryer and cook for 35 minutes.
6. Slice and serve.

Recipe Index

A

Asparagus Strata 20

Asparagus With Garlic 76

Air Fryer Reduced-sugar Cookies 79

Air Fried Lamb Ribs 49

Apricot-glazed Turkey Tenderloin 33

Apple Brussel Sprout Salad 72

Apple Chips 26

B

Baked Eggs With Mascarpone 18

Baked Potato Breakfast Boats 13

Balsamic Sautéed Greens 74

Banana And Walnut Cake 77

Banana Chocolate Muffins 84

Banana-pecan French Toast 19

Barbecued Chicken With Creamy Coleslaw 34

Basmati Risotto 67

Bacon And Pear Stuffed Pork Chops 52

Bbq Pork Ribs 29

Blackened Shrimp 61

Buttery Shortbread Sticks 81

Buttered Shrimp Fry 57

Bean Burritos With Cheddar Cheese 55

Beef And Pork Sausage Meatloaf 45

Beer-battered Fish And Chips 57

C

Cajun Fish Cakes 59

Cajun Chicken Drumsticks 42

Carne Asada Tacos 48

Cheddar Bacon Frittata 12

Cheddar Mushroom Cakes 70

Chicken Wings With Lemon Pepper 42

Chocolate S'mores 83

Chocolate Peanut Butter Bread Pudding 85

Chocolate Peanut Butter Molten Cupcakes 78

Classic Spring Rolls 46

Crumbed Golden Filet Mignon 53

Crunchy Pork Egg Rolls 31

Crusted Prawns 29

Creamy Tuna With Zucchinis 58

Creamy Cauliflower Puree 67

Crisp Paprika Chicken Drumsticks 39

Crispy Bacon Strips 27

Crispy Fish Sticks 16

Crispy Mustard Pork Tenderloin 47

Crispy Vegetable Nuggets 22

Crispy Paprika Chips 31

Crispy Chicken Cordon Bleu 36

Curried Brussels Sprouts 69

Cilantro-lime Chicken 37

Cinnamon And Sugar Peaches 28

Cinnamon And Pecan Pie 86

Cinnamon Pumpkin Cookies 83

Cinnamon-pear Chips 25

Corn With Coriander And Parmesan Cheese 24

D

Delicious Cheeseburger 50

E

Eggless & Vegan Cake 84

Elegant Pork Chops 46

English Pumpkin Egg Bake 12

Enticing Chocolate Cake 82

Erythritol Vanilla Butter Pie 86

F

Flavor Moroccan Harissa Shrimp 62

Flavorful Radish Salad 68

Fluffy Strawberry Cake 82

Fluffy Vanilla Butter Cake 87

Flounder Filets With Parmesan Cheese 61

French Mustard Chicken Thighs 35

Frittata 11

G

Garlic Lamb Rack 45

Garlic Steak With Cheese Butter 44

Garlic Edamame 26

Garlic Chicken Tenders With Pork Rinds 34

Garlic-basil Turkey Breast 33

Garlic-roasted Chicken With Creamer Potatoes 38

Grouper With Miso-honey Sauce 64

Ginger Mushroom Flounder 65

Ginger Salmon Fillet 59

Golden Pickles 75

Gorgonzola Mushrooms With Horseradish Mayo 71

H

Ham And Cheese Stromboli 50

Herb-roasted Vegetables 76

Herbed Pita Chips 23

I

Indian-style Chicken With Raita 41

Italian Dip With Cheese 24

Italian Frittata With Feta Cheese 21

Italian-style Honey Pork 53

J

Juicy Cheeseburger 54

K

Kale And Potato Nuggets 20

L

Lemon Parmesan Chicken 40

Lemon Cabbage With Cilantro 68

Lemon-pepper Chicken Wings 41

M

Marinara Pepperoni Mushroom Pizza 75

Marinated Pork Tenderloin 44

Mayonnaise Crab Dip 30

Maple Glazed Parsnips 71

Mushroom Frittata 15

Mexican Breakfast Pepper Rings 17

Mixed Pepper Hash With Mozzarella Cheese 17

Mozzarella Chives Omelet 14

Mozzarella Chicken And Pork Muffins 16

O

Old Bay Cod Fish Fillets 63

P

Parmesan Chicken Tenderloins 40

Parmesan Cod With Onion 62

Parsley Cabbage 69

Pasta Shrimp 58

Pumpkin Donut Holes 18

Purple Potato Chips With Chipotle Sauce And Rosemary 23

Pecan-crusted Turkey Cutlets 39

Pork Chops With Rinds 51

Pork Chops With Sage Leaves 47

Potatoes With Bacon 27

R

Rich Chocolate Cookie 87

Roasted Mushrooms With Garlic 30

Roasted Turkey With Veggies 43

Roasted Veggie Chicken Salad 38

S

S'mores 79

Snapper Scampi 60

Squash Chips With Sauce 22

Sriracha Golden Cauliflower 66

Strawberry And Peach Toast 11

Stir-fried Steak And Cabbage 55

Super Bacon With Meat 49

Super Veg Rolls 74

Sweet And Spicy Tofu 72

Sweet Orange Muffins 85

Sea Bass With Greek-style Sauce 56

Simple Fish Sticks 63

Simple Tomato Cheese Sandwich 15

Splenda Carrot Cake 80

Spinach And Cheese–stuffed Mushrooms 70

Spinach Egg Muffins 14

Spinach Omelet 13

Spicy Kale Chips With Yogurt Sauce 25

Spicy Cauliflower Roast 73

Spiced Rib Eye Steak 51

Spiced Shrimp With Zucchini 64

Spiced Pork Chops 48

Spiced Chicken With Pork Rind 35

Scallops With Green Vegetables 66

Scramble Casserole With Cheddar 21

T

Tandoori Chicken 37

Tuna And Fruit Kebabs 65

Turkey And Cranberry Quesadillas 43

Turmeric Cauliflower Patties 77

Typical Crab Cakes With Lemon Wedges 56

Typical Cod Nuggets 60

Tender Chicken With Parmesan Cheese 36

Tender Country Ribs 54

V

Vanilla Berry Cobbler 78

Vanilla French Toast Sticks 19

Vanilla Muffins With Pecans 81

Veggie Salmon Nachos 32

Vidalia Onion Blossom 28

W

Waffle Fry Poutine 32

Y

Yummy Apple Chips 80

Z

Zucchini Tots With Mozzarella 73

Printed in Great Britain
by Amazon